Modern Primitives: *Masters of Naïve Painting*

Modern Primitives:

Masters of Naïve Painting

Oto Bihalji-Merin

NOTED EUROPEAN ART CRITIC AND HISTORIAN

Harry N. Abrams, Inc.,   Publishers, New York

Library of Congress Catalog Card Number: 61–5784
Translated from the German by Norbert Guterman
Copyright 1959 in Germany,
by Verlag M. DuMont Schauberg, Cologne
Harry N. Abrams, Inc., New York
Printed and bound in West Germany

Table of Contents

List of Illustrations

André Bauchant

Rigaud Benoit

Emile Blondel

Camille Bombois

André Bouquet

Louis Augustin Dechelette

André Demonchy

Emerik Feješ

Jean Fous

10

Ivan Generalić

Asilia Guillen

Morris Hirshfield

John Kane

Dominique Lagru

Jules Lefranc

Orneore Metelli

Grandma Moses

Nikifor

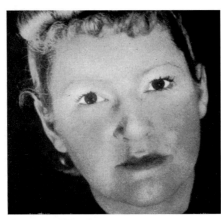

Gertrude O'Brady

Dominique-Paul Peyronnet

Niko Pirosmanoschvili

12

René Rimbert

Henri Rousseau

13

Jean Schubnel

Louis Séraphine

Patrick J. Sullivan

14

Camille van Hyfte

J. Antonio Velasquez

Mirko Virius

15

Miguel G. Vivancos

Louis Vivin

16

Sometimes I went back very far, further than the horses of the
Parthenon . . . to the wooden rocking horse of my childhood.

Paul Gauguin, Avant et après, *1903*

I The Utopia of the Primitive

Modern interest in primitive, archaic, and pre-historic art no doubt reflects a certain weariness of mechanized civilization and its excessive intellectualism. It also bears a relation to the infinite vistas that modern science has opened to us in its exploration of the atom and the cosmos. As, shaped by science, our picture of the universe has changed, becoming progressively more abstract, modern art, too, has extended the boundaries of the previously known. Artistic researches have entered many realms, and not the least important of these journeys into the unknown has revolved around earlier cultures in an attempt to penetrate the mystery of mankind's origins.

It was Paul Gauguin who launched our present-day exploration of "primitive" art, fancying the lands outside our cultural traditions as a utopia. He believed that the art of the primitive peoples, with their untapped reserves of strength, enthusiasm, and intensity, would inject new life into the dried-up sources of "civilized" art. His myth of the exotic utopia received its first formulation in his book *Noa Noa*. There followed, first, the discovery of Negro sculpture, some of it expressive of a stage in mankind's evolution known as the hunting culture, and, second, the appearance of a "naïve" or "popular" art among the inhabitants of our own jungles—the cities of modern civilization itself. These latter poets and dreamers still exist among us, producing their variously childlike or naïve landscapes of the soul, now gentle, now violent, unburdened by the weight of schools and traditions.

Such artists are not in flight from present time and place. Rather, what they do for us—unreflectively, unconsciously—is to rediscover the instincts that lie buried under the accretions of civilization. Much like those professional artists who have gradually eliminated representational elements from their works, these primitive artists are influenced by the course of modern knowledge, which has split our conception of the world into physical and visible elements on the one hand, and metaphysical, "existential" elements on the other. Both kinds of artists are searching for a deeper reality in terms of which art may bridge the gap between the visible and the invisible.

In his essay on Hugo von Hofmannsthal and his times, Hermann Broch speaks of the "realism" of primitive art, which tries to give a faithful image of reality, at the same time going beyond naturalism to the essence. "What the spontaneous beginnings of art reveal is that the artists' understanding is in organic unity with nature—theirs is the style of nature itself. The more art loses this, the less frequently it is characterized by the simplicity and directness of myth. We certainly do not find this organic unity with nature in Gauguin, but we do find it in Henri Rousseau; there is nothing of it in Joyce, but there probably is in Kafka." Broch might have mentioned Picasso along with Joyce and Gauguin as an artist led primarily by an intellectual vision to respect the primitive as embodying the essence of art. Whereas Picasso is continously, frenziedly engaged in extending the scope of his world to encompass the infinite, Henri Rousseau, working quietly, persistently, with workmanlike directness, endowed the reality that he alone discovered with a beauty as definitive as it is absurd.

Picasso, as we know, has often looked back to

the archaic forms of earlier epochs of art. He is the true—perhaps the last—heir to the ancient tradition. His imagination has more than once produced creatures charged with magic, with the power of the primitive gods. He not only discovered a rigorous realism in the abstract purity of Cubism, but went on to paint the Surrealist inspirations of his unconscious. But, whereas his work is rooted in boundless will and intellectual energy, in a conscious attempt to grasp the totality of life, Rousseau was at one with life. He lived it unconscious of his role as interpreter and prophet. He did not feel that what is remote in time is alien; he was at home in the remote, and, with the sureness of a sleepwalker, he *found* the emblems and the forms that other artists are forced to *invent*. In his virgin forests, we perceive the same magic forces that exist in the art of primitive peoples, but we also perceive the Cubists' sense of space and their fresh vision of the object.

In 1908, Rousseau made his famous remark to Picasso: "We are the two greatest painters of our epoch." This remark seemed ridiculous at the time—not only because Rousseau was poor and unknown, but because Picasso himself had most of his career still ahead of him. And yet, as it turns out, Picasso and Rousseau *are* two cornerstones of modern art.

Our need to rediscover the primal ground of being, to fill the vacuum left by the disappearance of gods and spirits with creative images for the living, underlies and accounts for the widespread interest displayed today in Rousseau and the other naïve painters. Rousseau was an outstanding artist, but he was not an isolated instance. His work paved the way for our acceptance of many other naïve artists.

They are known by various names in various places—"instinctive painters," "painters of the Sacred Heart," *"maîtres populaires de la réalité,"* "Neo-primitives," "Sunday painters." Whatever we call them, it is certain that, in an epoch of dissolving tradition and growing abstraction, they have come to stand for the reconquest of a lost reality.

The affinity of our present day for the sick in spirit in a certain sense has made the naïve painter of the twentieth century possible. In the stream of dilettantism and unschooled work, it may occasionally happen that merely inept or rudimentary art exists side by side with authentic naïve art. The amateur painter, in his search for perfection, may easily be led astray into false or spurious conceptions of art. The naïve artist, however, is trying to come to grips not so much with the forms of things as with the things themselves. The difficulties that he encounters in realizing his conceptions are less aesthetic than technical. For the naïve artist, the reality that he perceives and his idea of the picture are identical—just as among children and primitive peoples, who similarly do not distinguish between actual reality and their images of it.

Kandinsky coined the term "greater reality" to designate the naïve vision of things characteristic of modern primitives. Franz Roh, who has long been interested in naïve art, has talked of "magic realism." According to Werner Haftmann, "It is the naïve artist's will to definition that shows reality in its primeval manifestations, its 'primitive state,' its archaic 'original.'"

Labels in art have no more than an auxiliary function. Many artists began as naïve painters, but then, as they acquired skill and became conscious of their art, no longer qualified as primitives—in the process losing some of their original vividness and spontaneity. On the other hand, professional artists have passed from technical coolness and "scientific" precision to primitive, simple expression and the vivacity of the naïve.

Many artists have set out to rediscover a lost paradise where art shall no more be the concern of professionals, where the capacity to create images, like that of using words, shall be the common possession of all. Few, however, have found this paradise.

For art has primordial origins, to be found on the walls of your own children's rooms, just as truly as in the collections of ethnographic museums. Do not smile, reader—children are quite capable of inventing art, and there is something for us all to learn from this fact.

Paul Klee, 1912

II Art Outside Tradition

Paul Gauguin felt that the rational, intellectual edifice of civilization is a prison that prevents human nature from developing. Longing for the primeval, the barbaric, the primitive, he left Europe and went to the South Sea islands, where myth was still alive and union with the gods and nature still possible. Against the mechanics of civilization he set the spirit of nature; more highly than technical skill he valued primitive man's capacity for direct experience.

"Primitive art arises out of the spirit and makes use of nature. So-called 'refined' art arises out of sensations and serves nature. Nature is the handmaiden of the former and the mistress of the latter. This is how we have fallen into the terrible error of naturalism. Naturalism began in Periclean Greece.

Since then there have been many more or less great artists who attempted to combat this error with varying degrees of effectiveness. But the reactions they registered represent no more than occasional flashes of memory and reason; they never succeeded in arresting what was essentially an uninterrupted decadence century after century. The truly Primitive art, the art of the unspoiled mind—the most knowing of all—was that of Egypt. There was the key to it all. The only way of out our present abjectness is to go back to the principle of freedom and reason." (Morice, *Gauguin*.)

Since Paul Gauguin's discovery of the magic of primitive art, the civilized world has become more sensitive to the spontaneous creations of peoples living close to nature. Energies long suppressed by attitudes of positivism and skepticism have now reawakened and have sought to forge emblems and forms of more than merely aesthetic significance. But, as civilized men have become more and more fascinated with primitive peoples, the autonomous life and creative energies of these peoples have withered. With the impact of technology and imperialism, their gods and demons have lost their powers. The creative abilities of anonymous artists, scarcely less impressive than the powers of the trib-

al sorcerers, have become stunted. Robbed of the inspiration of magic and faith in the fetishes they created, these artists have been reduced to echoing traditional forms, manufacturing souvenirs for tourists, and practicing the techniques of mass production. But if the demons of the primitive peoples have lost their magic powers through contact with modern civilization, something of this lost animism has begun to turn up, transposed and modified, in the work of modern European artists. How this has come about and how modern art reflects these far-reaching influences are complex matters involving a great deal more than changes in form. The influence of Negro sculpture on modern European painting is well known and plain to see; an only slightly less obvious sign is the irruption of spirits and fetishes in Surrealist art. But perhaps the demonic powers are always with us, and are always to be found by men who search for them, as long as men have reason to fear themselves. There is a strain of despair as well as of hope in the search of cosmopolitan and metropolitan man for his origins. "The demonic realm is everything that urges man to destroy himself. The demons of the Church, of Freud, and of Bikini all bear the same features. The more new demons emerge in Europe, the more European art must recognize its kinship with cultures that were aware of the old demons." (Malraux, *The Psychology of Art.*)

At the turn of this century, many artists became conscious of the mysterious charm of Negro art, and as the relationship between man and his surroundings perceptibly weakened, and became more unnatural, artists attempted to revive the spirit that had been hidden beneath outward forms. Picasso turned from the transparent classicism of his figures of acrobats to the magic and archaic world of primitives. Derain, Matisse, and the Expressionists drew inspiration from African masks. The severely angular Bakota figures and the T-shaped stylization of eyes in the Pangora sculptures of Gabun influenced the formal inventions of the Cubists. Modigliani's portraits and sculptures were stimulated by the carvings of the Guro tribes of the Ivory Coast. Emil Nolde was deeply moved by primitive sculpture: "The artistic creations of the primitive peoples are the last remnants of a primeval art."

Whereas Gauguin sought to renew painting by contact with nature in the South Seas, Paul Klee found his inspiration not in the primitive but in the archaic and the unconscious. Psychoanalysis and paleontology were starting points for his particular delvings into childhood and artistic origins. Klee came to regard children's drawings as visual documents that, once deciphered, could lead us back to the wonderland of spontaneous poetic creation: "Art plays an unconscious game with the ultimate things, and yet it attains to them." (Klee.)

Artists who turned consciously to primitive and archaic art were in rebellion against civilization, with its soulless virtuosity and mechanized perfection. The art of children, of the insane, and of the naïve painters falls outside the context of historical civilizations.

When he paints, the child is still unaware of the principles of logical thinking and of the conventions for expressing the relations between ourselves and things. The discovery of signs, which is tantamount to becoming conscious of the world, takes place at the stage of childhood between speaking and writing. Spontaneous scrawls precede construction of images, the earliest symbols of knowledge. The images drawn by children—which are very similar to those produced by peoples without a written language—are the first articulations in the human individual of forms of communication.

As though equipped with his own X ray, the child

sees through walls and clothing, through all artificial divisions and compartments, and gives form to the life that they confine. In doing this, he adjusts proportions to his own measure, on the archaic principles of large and small, outside and inside. The child's vision is expressed in play and feeling, and the moment he goes beyond play and feeling he ceases to be an artist. "The child artist is like Kim, in his dreams a conqueror of cities, and also like Timur, whose empire vanished when he awoke." (Malraux.) Knowledge of cause and effect and the conscious pursuit of goals come to occupy the place formerly held by artistic creation. Dreams and visions are supplanted by systematic quotation from the card index of reality.

"The infinity of the preconscious childish soul vanishes, or, rather, survives with it. Therefore the residues of the childish soul in the adult include his best and his worst qualities alike, but in every case they obey the secret *spiritus rector* of our most significant actions and vicissitudes, whether we are conscious of this fact or not. It is they that endow the most insignificant counters in the game of life with the dignity of kings and queens, that transform an ordinary man from a father by accident into an all-powerful tyrant, or an ordinary women from an unwilling mother into a goddess of destiny. For behind every actual father there stands the eternal image of the father, and behind the passing figure of the personal mother there stands the magical figure of the mother pure and simple. The archetypes of the collective psyche, whose power is glorified in immortal works of art and in the fiery dogmas of religions, are also the powers that rule over the preconscious soul of the child." (C. G. Jung, Introduction to F. G. Wickes, *Zur Analyse der Kindesseele.*)

The art of primitive peoples expresses a developmental stage of mankind in creative terms. The art of the child, on the other hand, is a passing biological phase that no act of will can arrest. Both kinds of art stand outside their historical contexts, like the art of the insane, which, by breaking or dissolving the conventional relations between man and things, escapes the prison house of logic and sweeps aside the restraints of civilization. But the calligraphy of anxiety and the confused forms of madness cannot achieve creative continuity because their impulses derive from a sickness that also produces helplessness and withdrawal.

To be sure, it has always been difficult to distinguish with certainty between the normal and the abnormal, between healthy and morbid art. Today,

the demarcation line between the two can scarcely be drawn at all. Very little has been left of that sense of unity, created in the Renaissance, between the individual and the world that he explores and discovers. The artist of today does not think of himself as *homo universalis*. Out of harmony with his cosmos, he suffers from a sense of isolation and insecurity. His vision is not nourished in the public sphere, and he does not formulate it in a universally understood language. Very often it seems to be located in some twilight zone between dream and death, in some absurd, fantastic landscape. Hell is no longer a place of terror situated outside man's earthly existence, but is intimately and immediately present to him—an inner world of demons, nightmares, and hallucinations. The same disturbance in the relationship between individual and society, between man and things, characterizes the deranged mind and, in a sense, the modern artist's image of a disintegrated and dislocated world.

In his study on the sculpture of the insane, written in 1922, Prinzhorn analyzed the drawings of a mental patient in the following terms:

"Tulips and children's heads are arranged like apples in rows. The children in the back row came out larger than those in front. . . . The dark row of pine trees on top of the horizontal floor suggests different points of view. When we slowly examine each head in sequence, we sense, in the rigidity of the arrangement, a compulsion to repetition. A touchingly childish objectivity speaks in this crowded picture, in which the artist imagines that multiplicity can be rendered only by literal enumeration. This is certainly symptomatic of a childish mind, which expresses itself so candidly in consequence of illness. The picture brings peasant paintings to mind, as well as works by Henri Rousseau, the customs inspector who suddenly set himself up as painter. Even connoisseurs were fascinated by the utter simplicity of the images his charmingly childish nature gave birth to. His paintings and his life story make it highly probable that he should be classified as a quiet schizophrenic. This is rather compellingly suggested by his engaging gentleness and unworldliness in conjunction with certain visionary traits."

Not so many years have gone by since this analysis was written. Today, the man who wrote it would find in every exhibition the features that he classified as "schizophrenic." The abolition of perspective and anatomical structure, as well as displacement of foreground and background, is common in contemporary painting, and the decorative repetition of heads, which the psychiatrist thought of in terms of compulsion neurosis, reminds us of the expressive forms that have been generated by the spirit of technology and the collective psychology of the big-city dweller. And if we go so far as to call Rousseau's paintings schizophrenic, would we not be still more justified in applying this term to the many painters who deform visual appearance much more radically and are no less determined to put before us the full range of forms dictated by their inner vision?

Art has never confined itself to visual appearance, and has always been reluctant to submit to rules or conventions. It has often extended the boundaries of the normal to embrace the fantastic and the uncontrollable. Surely, Van Gogh's art is none the less great for reflecting hallucinations and the powers of darkness. Nor are Utrillo's gentle, luminous views of Paris less poignant once we know of his severe neurotic illness, or of his attempt to make his crumbling Montmartre walls more lifelike by pasting moss on them and mixing plaster with his paint, as a child might. Van Gogh and Utrillo were both self-taught painters. Utrillo is counted among the modern primitives, for his art preserves the naïve vision of

childhood. Van Gogh revealed a new relation between the self and the realm of things, and gave new meaning to the age-old value of innocence.

The only art that actually exists outside history, that reflects no biological stage of development and no psychic trouble, is the art of those who live outside time, unburdened by the knowledge or the sufferings brought by civilization—those who live naturally in the wonder of the world's first creation.

We are dealing with the last remnants of a vanishing collective soul, which, as in a dream, repeats over and over again the fundamental eternal elements of the human soul.

Carl Gustav Jung

III Primitive, Folk, and Naïve Art

Until the beginning of our century, the term "primitive art" has been used only to designate either the remains from prehistoric stages of the past, or the art of peoples living under primitive conditions in our own day.

The images produced by the prehistoric mind were expressions of collective experience; prelogical art was a formal language governed by instinct. Herbert Read describes this art as an activity of the senses, elementary and instinctual, like love, hate, and fear.

The magic practices of the prehistoric hunter were aimed at securing success in the hunt. The power of magic was as real to him as the ax that he had invented. His art revolved about animal forms. Whatever images of women have survived from that epoch emphasize attributes of fertility; the few human male figures are depicted in the role of hunters. Prehistoric art never departs from the practical sphere; the dark mysteries of birth and death are not touched upon. Magic antedates original sin.

The great revolution of prehistory came, perhaps, with the discovery that man does not live for the hunt alone, that not only are animals alive but all of nature. The courses of the stars and the succession of the seasons signal the rhythms of unknown forces —mysterious powers beyond the grasp of man. Useful or harmful, beneficent or maleficent, these powers were conceived of as spirits or demons, as the ghosts of the dead ancestors, and as the earliest gods.

The practice of magic—which continues to lead an underground existence to this day—encouraged witchcraft and sorcery. Mysterious new visions emerged, expressed in images and symbols. Thus the epoch of animism and totemism came about, of secret rites performed with masks, of the earliest notions of the soul—means by which man enters into communion with spirits, death, and the stars. Forces behind the visible surface of reality were imagined, and believed to govern life and growth. These hidden forces were the subject of animistic art.

The animistic artists among peoples still at a primitive stage of culture today are religious artisans. To them, art is not an aesthetic but a ritual activity. The perfection of the artistic form gives a work its magic power. These anonymous artist-magicians possess a certain affinity with the Byzantine painters of icons, who did not paint a sacred *image* but the sacred essence of the image.

When we reach the stage of folk art, magic and art alike give way to tradition and the communal spirit. The peasant artists who carry on a popular tradition are not sorcerers; they are not agents for trafficking with secret powers. Rather, they are the reverent guardians of a well-defined, traditional body of rules governing the art of the community.

The roots of folk art lie in the soil of tradition. This art signifies historical continuity, and is passed on from generation to generation. It does not rest upon individual taste, but, rather, upon custom and habit. As long as the community is secure, socially and spiritually, it provides a basis for the members to identify with one another, to maintain a feeling of kinship. Modern civilization dissolves all such older social structures. Folk art loses its spiritual significance, becoming a mere decorative souvenir of long-lost meanings. However, the anonymous forces that were embodied in folk art live on in a

Votive painting: The Pairing Off of the Beasts (Siegertsbrunn, 1838)

subterranean way. They re-emerge in individual artists after their social manifestations have disappeared. Folk art may, thus, lead to an individualistic art that combines the last emanations of the collective and the primordial with the timeless activity of play and the endless creativeness of children.

The most extensive collections of folk art are to be found in churches, monasteries, and cemeteries, most frequently as votive paintings and grave markers. The paintings, woodcarvings, metalwork, and embroidered objects are all quite small. They have been offered to some protective power in thanks for escape from peril. The dramatic event through which tragedy was averted—the last-minute rescue—is represented with the exactness of a country-fair photograph and with the naïveté of the believer in miracles. The figures and the costumes vary; the sentiment, which goes back to pagan antiquity and beyond, never.

Although the last of the Romantics made the attempt, they could not prevent folk art from dying out. The spirit of industrial development gradually undermined its aesthetic conceptions. The forms fixed by custom, by the artist's own memory, and by colorful traditions were gradually supplanted by a standardized taste reflecting current fashions. When outside interest in folk art was awakened, imitative or purely decorative art was the result. The artists who produced votive pictures, grave markers, religious paintings on glass, and decorations on peasant chests were followed by amateur and Sunday painters—the naïve artists proper—who, gifted in insight though technically unskilled, attempted to give visual expression to their basic experiences. In folk art there had been no clear-cut individualism: the anonymous communal tradition ends when the personality of the artist appears. The naïve painters rarely continue traditional patterns out of respect for their formal values, nor do they take the work of professional artists for a model. The naïve painters create spontaneously, untouched by conventions of style and unconcerned with public appreciation.

There is a certain parallel between folk sculpture and the sculpture of primitive peoples. The carved objects of herdsmen and peasants, their anthropomorphized shepherds' stocks and archaically ornamented pitchers, are reminiscent of Stone Age sculpture and of the clay pots and urns that served as primitive sacred vessels. Inaminate objects that they are, they are nonetheless animated with suggestions of the forms of human bellies, breasts, and necks—sometimes with painted ornaments suggesting eyes, heads, and necklaces.

One example of medieval folk art is the Bogomil stones in Bosnia and other parts of Jugoslavia. They are found along the roads, in the woods, and in the mountains. The oldest dates back to about the thirteenth century. They are a kind of children's drawing in stone, representing animals, hunting scenes, tourneys, and dances. They also evoke the magic rites of archaic cultures. With their curious ornamentation and figures of knights jousting with tremendous hands raised high, these stones possess the ponderous quality of the gigantic stone heads of Easter Island.

In the sixteenth century, another purely rustic sculptural art came into being and has survived down to our day: the grave markers in Serbian cemeteries. These spectral forms, primitive in appearance, use elementary symbolism in an attempt to make the ineffable visible. Among them are human figures with solar disks instead of heads, zoomorphic shapes, geometric figures, and realistic forms of peasants. These grave sculptures, which were originally painted, still show traces of color on the stone.

In spite of the decline of art among primitive peoples as a result of their contact with civilization, some worthwhile sculpture is still produced in a few regions where this contact has not been too intensive. These artists give visual form to their naïve dreams and legends with the help of the knife, the hammer, and the chisel.

The *santos*—carvings of saints—in the Spanish colonial style, such as those created by José Dolores

López of New Mexico, are contributions to the religious folk tradition and are remarkable for their fantasy and sense of form.

The sculptures of the Canadian Indian John Wallace are masterful variations on totem-pole art, as practiced by the Haida in the Pacific Northwest for centuries.

The handles of the guslalike instruments and the shepherds' stocks ornamented with human heads may be the last works of an anonymous peasant art in Europe. Nevertheless, in them the traditions of the past still reflect a certain vitality. Thus Petar Smajić, a Dalmatian peasant artisan, began his artistic career as a carver of guslas (single-stringed bowed musical instruments). He created austere, simplified human heads and figures, at once emotionally expressive and reminiscent of archaic sculpture.

Ordinary people all over the world, especially those who do not live in big cities—sailors, lighthouse keepers, and convicts as well as peasants and fishermen—shape naïve figures in cork, wood, shells, wax, and stone that are quite worthy of inclusion in any collection of modern primitive art. The Abbé Fouré spent many years chiseling his modern Cyclopes out of the steep cliffs near Saint-Malo; and the mail carrier Cheval, who is called "the Douanier of sculpture," spent decades building his magic castle, his *palais idéal*, in a village of Dauphiné, utilizing the accidental shapes of stones. Such artists were isolated eccentrics; it cannot be claimed for them that they led the way back to a collective anonymous folk art.

Do the naïve and self-taught painters constitute a new school, a separate branch of the richly diversified modern search for form? Have the modern primitives played a part in the dramatic development that has led from Fauvism to abstraction?

The naïve painters do not constitute a well-defined current within modern art. Their marvelously simple works occupy a place outside the intellectual debates of professional artists. The true naïve painter creates spontaneously and freely, at the dictates of his own feelings. The originality and poetic immediacy of such work delight by the unconscious sincerity with which private fantasies have been expressed. Not all the many and various works exhibited as neo-primitive or naïve art are true artistic expressions, but we sense vitality in all the tendencies and attempts. The "greater reality" that the genuinely naïve artist seeks has very deep roots. Naïve painting exhibits not only decorative simplicity and narrative primitiveness, but, above all, imaginative vividness and infinite delight in discovery. When it really possesses these qualities, it rises to the stature of authentic art. No well-informed person today would hesitate to rank Rousseau as an artist alongside Cézanne and Picasso.

However, our interest is not only in those artists who, by their genius, have singled themselves out above other naïve painters. There are a great many painters who turn to creative pursuits to relax from their exhausting occupations, and they, too, contribute to the reawakening of a lost art of spontaneity by the freshness of their conceptions and the directness of their statements.

Holidays, week-ends, and vacations are devoted to artistic creation. It is not surprising that some of the most important naïve painters did not begin their artistic careers until they were well along in life; the later years bring the leisure necessary for productive activities. The Douanier Rousseau was not able to devote himself full time to painting until he had retired on a pension. The same was true of Vivin, the post-office clerk, and of Hirshfield, who had been a manufacturer of boudoir slippers. Grandma Moses had to wait until the farm work had become too hard for her, to take up painting and find new meaning in life. To be sure, not all naïve painters are able to create works of permanent value. But when many persons are not content merely to enjoy art but also want to practice it, professional art is given a creative stimulus.

In a period when everything organic and alive is insufficiently valued, these naïve artists, with their childlike metaphors and their candid persistence, may succeed in breaking down the barriers that cut off art from the people and the people from art.

The artist, who in many ways resembles the child, can more easily than others attain to the inner core of things. Here lies the root of a great realistic art. The outer shell of the thing, when it is rendered with perfect simplicity, in itself sets off the thing from the realm of the practical and the useful, and helps to bring out its inner sound. Henri Rousseau, who may be called the founding father of such a realism, has shown us the way. The world . . . is a cosmos of spiritually active beings. Thus, dead matter is living spirit.

Wassily Kandinsky, 1912

IV Reality Renewed

Objects have all had to be discovered or invented by someone at some time. A four-legged chair incarnates the act of sitting, frozen into a material shape, but only as guided by living impulse. The hollowed-out pot was a creative development in imitation of the human belly. In tropical regions, pottery utensils were given the shapes of fruit. Trees became stakes on which dwellings were built, and these stakes eventually became pillars and columns. Every object embodies a living experience. Every object once possessed this kind of meaning, although often the meaning is lost or forgotten in the course of time.

About the turn of this century, man's interest extended to the extremes of microcosm and macrocosm, the infinitely small and the infinitely vast.

The stars and the atoms, domains par excellence of the inorganic and the nonhuman, now occupied the attention of the scientists and began to fascinate artists. In the study of man, interest shifted away from the conscious to the unconscious mind and from the present to the very earliest epochs. There was a similar movement away from logic toward the symbolic, the hidden, and the buried. As the cosmic and atomic horizons have broadened, the extent of what still remains to be known seems more unfathomable to man. The images of man and of things, as formulated in the Renaissance, have begun to break up, to disintegrate. The human form and the forms of things have become uncertain, blurred. Room must constantly be made in our understanding for new man-made objects and objects formerly outside human experience.

The generations that grew up after the turn of the century were skeptical about the naturalistic and positivist world picture. They could no longer swallow the predigested myths of classical nineteenth-century science. The deeper visions of specialized sciences afforded glimpses into the abyss, opened up virgin territories still unexplored. Seemingly established facts that had been taken for granted for generations were now put in question.

Science discovered that matter itself was subject to growth and change, and that atoms could be smashed. Einstein's theory of relativity, Planck's quantum theory, and De Broglie's theory of light paved the way for a new nonperspective conception of space-time, which superseded the world picture of classical physics. To the three Euclidean dimensions of space, time was added as a new, fourth dimension. The old maxim that nature makes no jumps, that only continuous development is possible, regarded as irrefutable since the time of Aristotle was swept aside by the quantum theory, in which matter, light, and energy are treated as essentially discontinuous. Just as the Renaissance enlarged two-dimensional space by means of perspective and thereby made it plastic, so the theory of relativity now altered the classical conceptions of space and time. Thanks to radium emanation and X rays, which pass through matter and make it seem transparent, it became possible to observe the birth and decay of the elements.

Modern psychology, meanwhile, has penetrated into previously unexplored regions of the psyche and deciphered the mythological content of memory. Freud's exploration of the unconscious and Jung's revelation of how the individual dream merges with the collective dream—his discovery of the domain of the archetypes—have opened new horizons and extended the range of artistic sensibility.

The glimpses into new infinities of space and time have had a serious effect on art. To give artistic expression to this reality, new techniques have been required. Beyond illusionistic space and aerial perspective there extends a landscape of distorted, dissolving forms, the landscape of non-objective art. The analytical experiments of Braque and Picasso, by an amazing process of synchronization, transformed the world into a mosaic of stereometric shapes. Objects were taken apart so they could be seen from the inside or viewed simultaneously from all sides, in a penetrating attempt to decipher them dialectically. Inspired by the extreme sensitivity of such modern instruments as giant telescopes and X-ray apparatus, artists have made their way into a completely unknown world of form, hitherto impenetrable to man. A new theory of perspective has made it possible to shift points of view or to adopt several points of view simultaneously. At the same time, to the Cubist imagination the world came to appear increasingly abstract, and the object more and more came to serve as a mere springboard for invention.

In 1910, Kandinsky turned his back on symbolism and painted his first nonobjective improvisation. As early as 1911, he produced abstract works made up of lines and networks of lines, and planes consisting of transparent areas of color, all of which revolve like stars around a firmament within themselves —echoes of cosmic harmonies. In a letter dated December 10, 1937, Kandinsky wrote to me: "There are still remnants of objects in my *Composition 1911*. This was followed by the purely abstract paintings of my so-called 'dramatic period.'"

Paralleling the explorations of Picasso, Braque, and Kandinsky, Paul Klee, who was repelled by the hollowness of modern mechanized forms of life, sought stimulation and inspiration in the vividness of prehistoric cave paintings and the rich fantasy of children. The simplicity of children's drawings, and the modern exploration of the unconscious and of the remote past, made possible by extremely subtle modern techniques, served as Klee's principal equipment when he set out on his own artistic researches into our archaic, utopian origins.

Casimir Malevich, in his book *The Nonobjective World*, says that art is no longer merely to provide illustrations for cultural history. "It will no longer have anything to do with the object as such, and believes it can exist in and for itself without the object, without 'the old reliable vital source.'"

At the very beginning of this period, when the representation of things began to seem increasingly stale and obsolete, Henri Rousseau found his own magical means of overcoming the soulless artificiality of the modern world. Things that, through habit and convention, had become invisible to man he brought back to life. Rousseau made a real reconquest of the world of things for art. To be sure, Rousseau had begun to paint a quarter of a century before the dissolution of the object. The year 1886, when he first exhibited at the Salon des Indépendants, saw the last exhibition of the original Impressionist group. However, Cézanne had already taken the first step away from the naturalistic visual system of the Impressionists toward a nonperspective, abstract mode of seeing. But, at this time, both Cézanne, who was attempting to reduce nature to pure form, and Rousseau, who, without a theoretical program and working merely from instinct, was reducing form to the magical reality and materiality of nature, were completely unknown.

Like a somnambulist, Henri Rousseau never deviated from his goal of giving concrete expression to his dreams and endowing the concrete with the reality of dreams. He thus anticipated the modern concept of reality as made up of dialectical tension between the visible and the conceivable, between vision and knowledge. Our sense of the real is enlarged by our awareness of the possible, and the utopian thus becomes a matter of immediate experience. Touched by his childlike magic, nature is transformed into a promised land. The act of creation is a kind of home-coming, and the things that modern civilization has reduced to mere commodities are restored to life. Modern man, after the long experience of being alienated from himself, thus discovers a new harmony.

A la fin tu es las de ce monde ancien
Bergère ô tour Eiffel le troupeau des ponts bêle ce matin
Tu en as assez de vivre dans l'antiquité grecque et romaine
Ici même les automobiles ont l'air d'être anciennes

Guillaume Apollinaire, Zone, 1913

[You have grown weary of a world effete
This morning Eiffel-tower shepherdess your flocking bridges bleat
Too long you lived with Roman and Greek
Here even the cars seem pseudo-antique]

Tr. W. J. Strachan, Methuen, 1948

V The Douanier Rousseau

He is not standing on the ground but hovering in mid-air, like some angel in a medieval Annunciation. High into the ragged clouds his head rises between two balloon forms, one earthly, one cosmic, a Montgolfier balloon and the sun. That was how Rousseau the Douanier portrayed himself (colorplate, page 41). Here he wears his black beret and a respectable black suit with a bit of white cuff showing—as is only proper. Behind him are one of the bridges over the Seine and a ship bearing pennants of all colors and nations. A couple is shown walking beside the river—tiny doll-like figures—looking at the ship, which appears just to have come in. Under the shimmering blue and green sky it seems a visitor from out of the vastness of time. In the background, the rectangular houses, with their vertical chimneys,

39

are lined up like soldiers to form an honor guard. Above them rises the lacy metalwork of the Eiffel Tower.

Did Faust stand thus at the bridge leading to the unexplored world beyond our understanding? The Douanier Faustus! This greatest of naïve artists holds his palette as emblem of his personal magic, and on it we read this inscription of loyalty and love: "Clémence et Joséphine."

What makes this painting so fascinating? The seriousness of the painter's expression, with his dark beard and mustache? the red patch under the beret which sets off the face? (The same red is repeated in the pennants, and among the color samples arranged on the palette as neatly as bonbons in a well-kept candy store.) Or is it the deep uniform black of the figure and the pale yellowish glow of the clouds, which has become softened with age?

Solemn, both touching and sublime, he stands before us as he saw himself and as we remember him: the solitary little man who surmounted ridicule and poverty alike by his own dedication and industry, to create the art that set off the creative explosion of painting in our century. Rigid and motionless as his figure may seem, at once in time and in eternity, like a clock without hands, there is no lack of symbols of movement to reflect the modern era: the incoming ship with pennants unfurled (as in one scene of his sentimental play, *A Russian Orphan's Revenge*), and his much-loved balloon, which is a bit of gray against the little clouds above, almost as the poet Christian Morgenstern might have composed the scene.

With the instinctive piety of the child, this self-portrait was placed within an airless world where architecture serves as a stage set: It is much closer to *trecento* paintings than to works in the mainstream of European art from the Renaissance to the Impressionists.

To look at this painting for any length of time is to be drawn ineluctably into all that remains of enduring wonder in the Paris of the turn of the century. No daring helmsman of the intellect will prove half so expert a guide as Rousseau, the steersman of the simple heart.

It is not possible to penetrate fully another man's intimate existence. You may open some secret doors, and even plumb some depths, but in the end you must recognize that you stand outside and see things from the outside. It would be tempting to invent stories to embellish the meager life of this

simple soul. He had qualities and attributes, of course. He was kindhearted, believing, even credulous. He had a mysterious ability to remain young and childlike. Fully susceptible to the charms of the trashy, he loved the most atrocious art of his period. He wrote poems with the same fervor with which he painted, and played sentimental airs on his violin with theatrical flourishes. Obviously he was a bit ridiculous, like a clown in the tradition of Charlie Chaplin.

If, instead of leafing through the chronicle of his life, we could turn over the pages of his dreams, we would find a different story. In this domain the Douanier proves a true visionary. Unexpectedly, he shows himself capable of breaking out of the conventions of the French lower middle class, of metamorphosing trash into poignant art. The commonplace conversation of a concierge becomes with him the sayings of a prophet: "I was recalling my great old friend, Henri Rousseau, that Homer of the portier's lodge, whose prehistoric dreams have more than once transported me to a place near the gods." (Max Beckmann, 1938.)

In the town of Laval, in northwestern France, on May 20, 1844, a son was born to the tinsmith Julien Rousseau and his pious wife Eléonore Guyard. At the christening, they gave him the euphonious name of Henri Julien Félix. As a boy, Rousseau must have found his father's workshop a magic place, with its glittering tin objects, the reddish-black darkness around the forge and its salmon-colored flames, the meaningful rhythms of the hammer striking, the silvery light filtering down from the skylight, and the soft glow of the lanterns. Tin gleams like platinum. It can be painted and made to look like marble. A palm made of papier-mâché can become a virgin forest, the dusty green velvet of a chair can become a lion crouching to spring.

Uhde was no doubt justified in disbelieving the story of Rousseau's military adventures in Mexico, although Rousseau himself vouched for them. The exotic glamor of the Mexican expedition may well have been one of the fantasies by means of which the painter veiled the humiliating circumstances of his humdrum life. Immersed in poverty and lack of worldly success, he projected childish daydreams of beauty and fame. His dreams were so intense and vivid that, in the twilight zone between fact and fancy, he sometimes crossed the boundaries of reality, and on one occasion convinced himself that the President of the Republic had invited him to an evening reception but that the rude doorman had turned him away because of his shabby clothes.

Rousseau's friends took advantage of his naïveté and credulity, and played practical jokes in dubious taste. On one occasion, they brought to his studio a man whom they falsely introduced as Puvis de Chavannes, and who proceeded condescendingly to praise Rousseau's paintings. On another occasion they introduced him to a man who looked like the State Secretary for Fine Arts. Rousseau was overjoyed at this recognition by the government, to the great amusement of the pranksters.

Rousseau took part in the war of 1870–71 as a sergeant. One of his paintings, *The Artillerymen* of 1894, evokes this period; the same may be true of *War* (page 158) painted in 1895. After his discharge from the army, he married Clémence Boitard. At that time, he was employed by a lawyer specializing in collections. According to Rousseau's niece, Madame Jeanne Bernard, the kindhearted artist found it intolerable to have to seize and impound the furniture of those who were unable to pay their debts. A cousin of his wife's procured for him the post of second-class clerk in the Paris customs service. He probably did not prove too efficient at this job, and was assigned to less exacting duties. But

Rousseau always firmly believed that his superiors acted out of kindness, so that he could have more time to paint. He performed his duties at the Porte de Montrouge, on the Tournelles bridge, and at the Porte de Meudon. Many of the landscapes that we admire today were first sketched while he was on duty in these places. It is reported that he spoke very little and rarely confided in any of his colleagues.

Of the nine children born to him and his wife, eight died. One daughter survived him. About 1884, he was granted a pension, which made it possible for him to devote himself more fully to painting.

On his door at No. 2a in the Rue Perrel there was a sign: *Cours de diction, musique, peinture et solfege* ("Lessons in recitation, music, painting, and sight singing"). In his little apartment he led a curiously double life. This shy, unworldly little man, who seemed swallowed up in the bustling indifference of the big city and who during his lifetime was mostly ridiculed or admired only in an ironic vein, was at the same time an austere artist firmly convinced of his creative mission. Standing in front of the life-size portrait of his dead wife, Clémence, he would play the violin or the flute; he also composed music and wrote poems and plays. In his painting, however, all the elements of his emotional life attained their most perfect expression. The daughters of the artisans and storekeepers of the quarter of Plaisance came to his apartment for their violin or singing lessons. He also had pupils whom he instructed in drawing.

In this apartment he met the swindler Sauvaget to discuss a naïve scheme that eventually involved the unsuspecting artist in a criminal charge, so that he was held for some time in the prison of La Santé. His letters from prison, which give us a glimpse into this questionable episode, are of great value to art historians.

Today, when Rousseau's works are jealously preserved in the Louvre—the ultimate tribute to any artist—it is not easy to grasp why Rousseau did not have more success during his lifetime. Rousseau's compositions of familiar and fantastic scenes, both his mysterious and magical landscapes, figures, and visions, are so much a part of us today that we can scarcely understand how the critics or the public could ever have heaped ridicule on them.

One of the two paintings that he exhibited at the Salon des Champs Elysées in 1885 was slashed with a penknife by an angry viewer. His works were, for the most part, hung so that they would be as inconspicuous as possible, because the sponsors of the exhibition—they did not function as a jury—were ashamed of them. But Rousseau's ironic admirers went out of their way to find his exhibits, and never failed to have a good laugh when they did.

However, a few sensitive and perspicacious artists recognized the special qualities of these unusual paintings. Paul Signac, one of the founders of the Salon des Indépendants, asked Rousseau to join the group that he headed with Maximilien Luce. From 1886 to his death, Rousseau exhibited regularly with this group, except for a brief interruption. Pissarro, Redon, and Gauguin became interested in him at an early date. In 1890, when some members of the Salon voted to exclude Rousseau, Toulouse-Lautrec came to his defense.

The following year, when Gauguin embarked for Tahiti, Rousseau painted the *Portrait of Pierre Loti* (page 161), and his first exotic scene, *Storm in the Jungle.* Henri Perruchot, author of an outstanding biography of Rousseau, is right in maintaining that these two works are related. Pierre Loti, member of the French Academy, was the troubadour of exoticism. It is possible that Gauguin was influenced by Loti's novels in his decision to go to the South

Seas. The cult of faraway lands lapped by the waves of alien oceans, the attempt to get back to the primitive sources of life, formulated by Loti, constituted a rejection of conventional society and reflected a desire to escape from it.

In taking Loti as his model, Rousseau was not inspired by these intellectual considerations. He painted Loti, whose face he obviously knew only from magazines and newspapers, as the interpreter of the dreams of the age. He managed to perceive all that lay beneath the bourgeois stolidity of Loti's features.

The writer and a cat, painted with sculptural hardness and placed in the foreground in a childlike manner, look out at us gravely from the picture. The pink face under the red fez is enlivened with a curled mustache. The dark cat has horizontal white stripes, and the man wears a dark sweater, from which the white collar and cuffs of his shirt appear. The hand, with a ring on the little finger and holding a cigarette, is held forward conspicuously to provide a counterbalance to the cat; similarly, the acacia tree against the transparent sky balances the organ pipes of the factory chimneys. Rousseau's famous and greatly admired contemporary reminds us of the subjects of his novels by the exotic touches in his costume. The portrait has been executed with great meticulousness. Its gravity and sincerity catch the touch of vanity that lies under the mask of dignified composure.

Georges Courteline, the playwright and humorist, bought this painting for his private gallery of horrors. He saw only the grotesque and comical elements in it.

The man who first took a serious interest in Rousseau was Alfred Jarry, the poet and author of the play *Ubu Roi*. Jarry was about twenty at the time, a fantastic young man deeply in love with the dream world of Rimbaud and Lautréamont. Henri Rousseau's extralogical alchemy as an artist appealed to his own rebellious nature and grotesque inspiration. Rousseau and Jarry were both natives of Laval. The unaffected candor of this former customs clerk, who not only painted his incredible pictures but insisted on exhibiting them in public, impressed Jarry more than the artistic qualities of the works, which he could scarcely grasp. It was enough for him that most people scoffed at Rousseau, and Jarry sprang enthusiastically to his defense. To demonstrate the independence of his opinions to his contemporaries, he commissioned Rousseau to paint his portrait with his favorite animals, an owl and a chameleon. The portrait was exhibited at the Salon des Indépendants in 1894. But Jarry grew tired of it; he cut out the head, and eventually the whole work was lost. According to Francis Jourdain, the well-known critic, Jarry, who was fond of guns, used the head of the portrait as a target for revolver practice.

The portrait of Pierre Loti already possessed the specific qualities that Rousseau displayed sixteen years later, toward the end of his life, in his portrait of the art dealer Brummer. The Brummer portrait, too, goes beyond the personality of the model. Enthroned in a wicker chair, under the ornamental foliage of fantastic trees, Brummer sits in rigid meditation, resembling a Byzantine Christ of the eleventh century. Related in character is the double portrait of Apollinaire and his Muse, painted in 1909. It pictures Apollinaire the poet as poet, so to speak, with the definitiveness of an emblem. The subject is shown holding a quill pen and a scroll of paper, while his Muse, the painter Marie Laurencin, guides him with a hand raised prophetically. They stand in a bower of greenery, under trees; a wall of red, pink, and white carnations symbolically protects the poet from the outside world.

Wilhelm Uhde tells us that Rousseau, when he was tired and discouraged, would find fresh confidence by looking at his portrait of his first wife, Clémence. In her broad-sleeved velvet dress, her right hand on hip, an umbrella in her left hand, a tiny cat at her feet playing with a ball of yarn, Clémence makes a monumental figure presiding over Rousseau's life. The narrower are life's limits, the vaster is the dream—especially the dream of love. Who, after all, was Dulcinea? All we know of her is the ideal image retained by Don Quixote.

Rousseau also painted his second wife, Rosalie Joséphine Noury, who worked in a stationery shop. We see them standing together in a garden behind flowering bushes, in their black Sunday clothes. The painter looks serious, his wife affectionate and devoted. But, above the couple, as though above time in some eternal realm, a second double portrait appears: Rousseau, looking somewhat different in an old-fashioned beard, and Clémence, his first wife. This consciousness of the past is intimately present, composed of all that is really permanent in life; it embodies the true meaning of Bergson's *durée réelle*.

After Joséphine's death, late in his life, Rousseau became involved in a petit-bourgeois drama centered on the person of the fifty-four-year-old Léonie, a saleswoman in a department store. The old man was still young in heart and still worshiped at love's sacred fires. But Léonie's father opposed the marriage. The Philistine's objections were based on Rousseau's poverty and, even more, on his ridiculous and unprofitable devotion to art. It was in this connection that Rousseau obtained from Uhde and Vollard the document that has since become famous, certifying the honorable character of his profession and the value of his works. Despite the document, however, the ceremony of betrothal he so yearned for was to become a Chaplinesque farce of disappointment.

Yet another woman's name appears in Rousseau's life—Jadwiga. Did he ever know a Jadwiga? or was she merely a fantasy? In 1910, when he exhibited *Jadwiga's Dream* (colorplate, page 49) he attached the following poem to the frame:

Yadwigha, dans un beau rêve,
S'étant redressée doucement,
Entendait les sons d'une musette
Dont jouait un charmeur bien pensant,
Pendant que la lune reflète
Sur les fleuves, les arbres verdoyants,
Les fauves serpents prêtent l'oreille
Aux airs gais de l'instrument.

[Yadwigha, peacefully asleep,
enjoys a lovely dream:
she hears a kind snake charmer
playing upon his reed.
On stream and foliage glisten
the silvery beams of the moon;
and savage serpents listen
to the gay, entrancing tune.]

Tristan Tzara believes that Jadwiga was a Slavic woman who was close to Rousseau and inspired him to write his play *A Russian Orphan's Revenge*, but, according to H. Perruchot, she was just as much a fiction as the expedition to Mexico. He holds that she may have been an *imago* of Rousseau's first wife, Clémence; but surely, if this had been the case, *Jadwiga's Dream* would have been a very different picture.

She lies naked on the red sofa that was part of the furniture in the Rue Perrel. The setting is a thick cluster of intertwined giant lilies, lianas, ferns, and other lush tropical foliage invented by the painter. A dark-skinned figure is playing a flute, while tigers, elephants, and birds peep out from the thick jungle. The magic of this painting is such that the Surrealist presence of the red sofa in the forest seems altogether right and natural. Rousseau always employed elements of reality in his waking dreams. He believed so sincerely in his vision that he persuades us that the fabulous scene has been actually viewed by the painter through field glasses. An unreal time and space are transformed into a precisely localized real place. Faith, which makes all things possible, has transmuted the typical petit-bourgeois ideal picture into the simple, delicate poetry of a folk song.

Ambroise Vollard, who bought *Jadwiga's Dream*, reports an interesting conversation he had with Rousseau, in his *Memoirs of an Art Dealer*. When he asked the artist why everything in this painting seems so real, Rousseau said, "Because I study nature."

For the primitives and for children everything is real, and grown-up "civilized" reality is magically transfigured by their poetic innocence.

Rousseau's finest painting of a woman is without doubt the *Sleeping Gypsy* of 1897 (page 160). In the moonlit wilderness we see a dark-faced woman lying on the ground in a picturesque costume. Is she only dreaming, under the cold green sky, that the terrifying mythical lion is leaning over her? The great silence of sleep and the silence of the desert, the dreamy depths of primordial existence, are here pictured with unconscious genius. Although a number of the details are meticulously realistic, this is not a genre painting, nor does it tell a story—it is the eternal essence of the dream and its age-old symbolism.

"The secret imagines it is alone and sheds all disguises," Jean Cocteau said of this work. "The gypsy sleeps with eyes half open. . . . How can I describe the motionless figure and its flowing movement, this flow of oblivion? It reminds me of Egypt, where eyes were kept open even in death, like those of the diver under the surface of the ocean. . . . Where do such things drop from? The moon? . . . Moreover, it is perhaps not without its point that this artist, who never neglected a detail, shows us no tracks in the sand, no imprint near the sleeping feet. The gypsy has not come here. She is here. She is not here. She is at no human place. She is one of those who live in mirrors."

Neither the woman nor the lion has come from anywhere else to this sacred landscape. They have always inhabited this mythical site of utopia. The deep space of the landscape holds all the boundlessness of being, and the green river between the

desert and the moonlit mountain flows like infinity. Like an island in space, man is situated in the inner monologue of his existence between the deserts of sky and earth. But the totality of the vision needs symbolic forms materialized in supernatural hardness—the pitcher and the mandolin. Henceforward, these two objects were to haunt the spaces of the Cubists and the dreams of the Surrealists.

In order fully to understand Rousseau's longing for the exotic, for the invention or discovery of landscapes never before glimpsed or visited, we must visualize the constriction of his petit-bourgeois environment, the disillusionments of poverty, the hollowness of the conventions which ruled his everyday life. A dog-eared collection of picture magazines, family newspapers, advertising posters, and catalogues, and a few books with illustrations of plants, occasionally served to stimulate his imagination, in the sense of giving him a take-off point. By this means he could fly from the frustrations of ordinary life to the imaginary shores of untouched jungles, spy out the secrets of tropical storms, witness the struggles of powerful beasts, and listen to the silence and the voice of the virgin forest.

About twenty years before Picasso was launched in his Negro period, Rousseau demonstrated the richness and primitive force of visual imagery. What is important in his art is not the geographic or ethnographic unfamiliarity of his landscapes. African and Oriental motifs are also to be found in Delacroix, Fromentin, Ingres, and Matisse. The world discovered by Rousseau—this Columbus among naïve painters—is the paradise of the primitive. His plants and fabulous creatures, his human figures and his skies—all of them are product of a childlike imagination and an uncomplicated poetic mind.

Nor is his a paradise of gentle peace and meditation. In the depths of Rousseau's jungles, fearful struggles are going on. Eve and the Serpent, temptation and sin, are also present in these flowering gardens of eternity. In the magical panopticon of his imagination, predatory beasts slink through the high ferns. A lion is tearing a gentle antelope to pieces (page 162). A Negro is attacked by a leopard. A native struggles with a gorilla. The screechings of monkeys and flamingos mingle with the color dissonances of innumerable greens. And the penetrating notes of the flute cast a spell over the forest. The naked black figure of the snake charmer stands against the light, her back turned to the luminous green sky and the shimmering river. Writhing snakes are emerging from the dank vegetation, preparing to dance. A slippery necklace, they wind about this Eve's shoulders and breasts. What is the meaning of this picture? The snake charmer's eyes are glowing mysteriously in her dark face. The fantastic heart-shaped leaves, the white-and-yellow-veined bushes with sharp points, and the foliage of the prehistoric trees appear as though molded in glass or carved out of some hard substance. The plants, the water, the moon, and the pink flamingo are all held spellbound by the snake charmer's song.

For Rousseau, the exotic is simply the poetic, no more and no less. Objects are painted in meticulous detail, but these trees and flowers do not belong to any known botanical species. Whether he was inspired by plants in the Jardin des Plantes in Paris or by tapestries at Angers is a purely academic question. Rousseau does not copy or imitate the forms of either art or nature. His proportions are not those of the visible world; they are integral components of his own vision. He subordinates detail to his composition as a whole. The plant life, in these pictures, constitutes a decorative, stylized, hitherto unseen landscape of his own invention, monumental in its harmony.

Rousseau's exoticism is not expressed primarily in his choice of subjects. His landscapes and views of cities in France bear the imprint of primitive strangeness no less than his fantastic locales. The trees in his picture of the Promenade of Vincennes have a magical character; they are painted leafless and without the luminous envelope of the Impressionists. In the *Paysage des Fortifs*, nature has been geometrically simplified, and gives the effect of a deliberately constructed composition. In *Stone Quarry* the walls rise nakedly, reflecting the sadness of the overcast sky. In *Spring in the Valley of the Bièvre* the natural data have been altered to fit an inner image: the shapes of the trees and the foliage are no less "fictitious" than those of the exotic forests. In the large landscape of 1906, called *Summer*, we find, along with instinctive simplicity of vision and meticulous craftsmanship in execution, a suggestion of the elemental treatment of forms that was a short time later to become a goal of the Cubists. Behind and beneath the play of forms—yet not consciously realized for the most part—there is a legendary harmony linking man with the animals and with nature.

The *View of the Rue Malakoff*, with its rectangular groups of houses and its childlike treatment of vegetation, is a decorative construction, contrasting the vertical accents of the gas lamps and the massive telegraph poles with the loosely stretched wires, the red and brown strips of the cultivated fields, and the straight lines of the street where women in gigantic yellow hats are strolling under a gray sky. Similarly, the *View of the Footbridge at Passy*, which shows the Trocadéro and the Eiffel Tower, and the *Conquest of Air*, which contains items of modern technology, have the same primitive, exotic quality.

Rousseau loved people and things. He felt a bond of solidarity with everyday objects. A woman's hat, a kerosene lamp, a vase—for him such things possessed a startling individuality in addition to their familiar appearance. The artist invested these humble inanimate objects with a poetic expressiveness, at once gay and grotesque. His magic world was built of simple things, seemingly dead, that he brought to life and human significance.

The artist was also very fond of the most striking technological developments of his time—the balloons known as *montgolfiers*, dirigibles, and the first biplanes of the Blériot era. In his paintings, these machines hover motionless in a frozen sky, like motorized angels. Rousseau treats such instruments of mobility without regard for their mechanical function. Dashing cabriolets, galloping horses, airplanes, dancers, and ballplayers are all set down as though congealed in time and space—in an altogether unclassical manner, as though an art of light and movement had never existed. The *Ballplayers* of 1908 (colorplate, page 53), which has been misnamed "Football Players"—a social document so far as the subject is concerned—is fascinating for its almost spectral treatment of an everyday scene. In a clearing in the woods—or is it an athletic field?—four men, perhaps only half the number of players involved, are shown playing ball. Rousseau is supposed to have portrayed himself twice in this painting. The ball is suspended in mid-air above the players who, wearing zebra-striped sweaters, are trying to catch it. Their postures are curiously twisted; they are captured at the moment of jumping, as in a snapshot. Despite the frenzied action, the men, with their pointed mustaches and neatly combed hair, are depicted as meticulously as though they had posed for the painter in his studio. The harmony of the tobacco-brown trees and the light-blue sky is echoed in the sweaters. The total effect of the colored space raises the banal sports event to the dignity of a modern ritual.

Henri Rousseau: Ballplayers

The same impression of time standing still is conveyed in *The Christening*, also called *The Family*, which shows the group standing in front of the house. The men, with glasses of wine, stand on one side. The women stand on the other, with the children in between. While many naïve painters portray country life in its active aspects, Rousseau liked to portray the common people in their moments of leisure. He was thoroughly familiar with their ways—he himself was one of them—and his scenes of their life, depicting family celebrations, such as christenings, weddings, or Sunday picnics in gardens and villages, are delightful. *A Country Wedding* (page 159) shows the bride, the bridegroom, and the members of the family standing in their clean, freshly ironed clothes, while the old folks are seated. The setting is enhanced by some unusual trees—chestnut trees that look like fig trees and acacias. Rousseau is said to have taken a corner of the Jardin des Plantes for his setting. The father of the bride is holding the marriage contract; the mother is touching the bride's wedding gown, which she probably sewed herself. All the figures wear their Sunday best and stand as though posing for a photograph. Everything is exactly as it should be, as proper as any man of the people—or any bride—would wish.

Père Juniet's Cart gives a delightful picture of the pleasures of a Sunday outing. We do not know whether the family in the two-wheeler is merely out for a ride or is on the way to visit friends in a nearby village. The members of the family, the dapple-gray horse (whose expression recalls that of donkeys in medieval monastery murals), and the two little dogs all stand still as if posing for a photograph. The men, as is proper, sit in front, and the women and children are in the back, stiff and solemn.

Rousseau had set ideas about the duties of a citizen. These come out in his portrayal of ordinary life within his own social group—the world of the lower middle class. His paintings depicting public events—*A Century of Independence*, *Liberty Invites the Artists* (page 163), *War*, and *Peace*—reflect his republican patriotism, his humanitarianism, and his cosmopolitanism.

Why, in 1894, did he paint *War* (page 158)? Did he have in mind the distant war then being waged by Japan against China for the possession of Korea? Actually, this painting represents no specific war, but war as such, the idea of war. We do not know what inspired him to paint this work. He himself wrote: "War goes by in its grisly way, leaving despair, tears, and destruction in its wake."

The painting shows a landscape of mutilated bodies, splintered trees, and a wildly galloping horse mounted by a strange figure, the Fury of War. This rider, brandishing a sword in one hand and a smoking torch in the other, is conceived very naïvely, almost childishly, and was probably inspired by conventional romantic allegories. A dwarf, wearing a ragged white garment and mounted on her demonic steed, she has lost all naturalistic features. Rhythm, color, and the composition as a whole transform her into a hallucination, at once grisly and absurd. This Fury of War has nothing of the noble grandeur of romantic attitudes toward death. What could the artist have had in mind when he imagined this childlike creature with a mask for a face and hair that streams in the wind? Under the horse's hoofs and across the entire width of the picture lie the livid corpses, the decaying bodies of the dead, which have been rendered with unsparing meticulousness. Behind a grid of leafless branches a lemon-yellow expanse of sky gradually approaches a silky blue. Cottony pink clouds suggest the flames of war.

The inexorable stillness of death, the frozen movement, the hardness of outlines bring to mind Uccello's harshly plastic, ritualistic *Battle of San Romano*. The nightmarish myth of *Guernica*, upon which Picasso lavished his most imaginative pictorial symbols, is closely related to this forceful picture, which reduces war to its simplest terms.

This painting of Rousseau's is complemented by the work of 1906 or 1907, entitled *The Representatives of Foreign Powers Arrive to Salute the Republic and to Sign the Peace*. The actors in this scene are lined up like soldiers for a military review. The Frenchmen, with their mustaches, long sideburns, and nineteenth-century civilian clothes, are holding symbols of peace in their hands, and are being greeted by the Angel of Peace with an outstretched olive branch. The sovereigns are in uniform, as is proper, and bedecked with medals. They include Tsar Nicholas II of Russia, King Edward VII of England (or is it George V?), and several others. There are also boyars and Oriental potentates, with pointed hats, turbans, and sombreros, all of them gathered to draw up a treaty of peace. A heraldic lion is also present. The happy citizens, including pigtailed Chinese as well as inhabitants of the Paris *faubourgs*, dance around a bronze monument to celebrate the festival of peace on earth and love among mankind.

Many critics speak of Rousseau's "development,"

probably because it has become customary to assume that every artist "develops." And, indeed, it may be possible to discover technical accomplishments in Rousseau's later works that are without parallel earlier. But such changes would scarcely prove essential, and certainly do not mark a deepening or improvement of his art. As early as the *Landscape at the Edge of the Woods*, painted in 1866, all visual elements incidental to his theme have been deliberately omitted. Visible nature is enriched and transfigured by poetry. In the portrait of *The Artist's Wife in the Garden*, dated 1890, and in the *Self-portrait with Palette* of the same year, the elements of natural appearance are subordinated to a profound conception, just as they are in the much-admired *Portrait of Joseph Brummer* of 1909. To be sure, the *Snake Charmer* of 1907 and *Jadwiga's Dream* of 1910 are the masterpieces of his old age. But the same magical power and vivid poetic quality, the same somnambulistic sureness of composition, are to be found in the *War* of 1894 and the *Sleeping Gypsy* of 1897.

The specific features of Rousseau's brushwork, the clarity and hardness with which he shapes his human figures, animals, trees, and foliage, are present from the beginning. People and things are not experienced by him in light and movement. Not only the features visible to the eye, but also those felt or intuited are integral elements of his inspiration. Like the Byzantine painters of icons, Rousseau identifies the colors and forms of his works with the things themselves. From the very outset, Rousseau is fully Rousseau. His vision, when he set out to record it for the first time, was just as mature as it ever would become.

Henri Rousseau died poor and alone, in the Hôpital Necker in Paris, in 1910. Robert Delaunay and Queval, Rousseau's landlord, bought a tombstone. Apollinaire jotted down an epitaph in pencil, and the sculptor Brancusi and the painter Ortiz de Zarate together incised it on the stone three years later, preserving the poet's handwriting:

Gentil Rousseau tu nous entends
Nous te saluons
Delaunay sa femme Monsieur Queval et moi
Laisse passer nos bagages en franchise à la porte du ciel
Nous t'apportons des pinceaux des couleurs des toiles
Afin que tes loisirs sacrés dans la lumière réelle

Tu les consacres à peindre comme tu tiras mon
    portrait
La face des étoiles

[Gentle Rousseau you can hear us
We salute you
Delaunay his wife Monsieur Queval and myself
Let our luggage pass duty-free through the gate
    of Heaven
We are bringing you brushes paints and canvas
That you may spend your sacred leisure hours
Painting in the light of truth eternal
The face of the stars
As you once painted my portrait]

Since then a great deal has been written about
Henri Rousseau, at first only by men of letters. But
while his works were still being both openly and
secretly sneered at, the personal legend of this
disarmingly innocent and gentle old man kept
growing. Apollinaire called him "the angel of
Plaisance," and devoted to him these poignant lines
in his poem *Recollection of the Douanier:*

Un tout petit oiseau
Sur l'épaule d'un ange

Ils chantent la louange
Du gentil Rousseau

Les mouvements du monde
Les souvenirs s'en vont
Comme un bateau sur l'onde
Et les regrets au fond

Gentil Rousseau
Tu es cet ange
Et cet oiseau
De ta louange

[A tiny bird
On an angel's shoulder—
They sing in praise
Of the gentle Rousseau

Movements of the world
Memories fade away
Like a ship on the wave
Its burden sunk to the bottom

Gentle Rousseau
You are this angel
And this bird
Who praise you]

The poets who wrote about Rousseau emphasized his intuition and his innocence, rather than his knowledge and skill, and his artistic qualities were overlooked. In the legend created and spread by Apollinaire and his friends, Rousseau had become a medium for the collective unconscious, which was supposedly to have created his work.

Today, quite the opposite view is gaining ground. Once divested of the nimbus of naïveté, which stamped him as shepherd to the flock of "the painters of the simple heart," Rousseau has come to be considered one of the great masters purely and simply for his qualities as an artist.

Rousseau is actually both a naïve genius and a great artist. For a long time he was a hero of legend, looked upon as all but the originator of modern art. But his greatness as a painter does not consist merely in the excellence of his visual observation; it consists also in the spirit of his visions. He not only anticipated much in the future development of modern painting in France and elsewhere; he also opened new horizons to humanity.

. . . another tradition has been disclosed by historical investigation, namely, the fifty thousand years of primitive art. In the light of this tradition, Picasso, Klee, and Miró are linked with the artist of Combarelles and Altamira, Rouault with those of Saint-Savin, Bombois with the steatopygic sculptors and draftsmen of the Magdalenian epoch, Matisse with the art of Knossos and the Etruscan frescoes, Vivin with the illuminators of Indochina and the designers of the Bayeux tapestries, and Séraphine with the woven fabrics of Ispahan. . . .

Henri Bing-Bodmer

VI   The "Sacred Heart" Group and Others, in France

I was given my first real insight into naïve art in the house of Wilhelm Uhde, in the Faubourg St.-Germain. There I saw for the first time the world of Vivin and Séraphine, of Bombois and Bauchant—four of Uhde's "Sacret Heart" group. I was deeply moved by the supernatural flowers of Séraphine's imagination—flaming bouquets embroidered in ecstatic colors: dazzling yellows, disquieting greens, peaceful autumnal wine-reds, and naïvely pious, luminous turquoise blues.

Séraphine Louis, sometimes called Séraphine de Senlis, was born at Assy (Oise) in 1864. Neither as a girl growing up in the country and tending farm animals, nor later as a domestic servant, did she study painting. Just when did she begin to translate her dreams and desires into colors and forms? Why did she do it? We know very little about the inner drama of her humble existence, and we would know even less than we do about her art had not fate accidentally brought her together with the man who, deeply impressed by Rousseau's fantasies, was hot on the trail of modern primitives.

In 1912, Wilhelm Uhde went to Senlis for a rest. Senlis is a quiet old town, not too far from Paris but far enough not to have been spoiled by it. Every morning an elderly woman came to clean his flat. Uhde scarcely took any notice of her. Then, one day, while calling upon his neighbors, he noticed a still life of apples. Struck by the picture, he asked who had painted it. "Why, it's your servant, Séraphine," he was told. Up until then she had worked entirely on her own. Now Uhde saw to it that the entrancing bouquets of flowers grew into enormous, fantastic trees. He got Séraphine the large canvases that she had long been wishing for. She now produced a series of endless variations on a single theme—her strangely Luciferian bouquets (colorplate, page 61; page 168)—and still lifes of the sensuous, sacred fruit of paradise that she dreamed about in her little room.

Uhde tells how jealously Séraphine guarded the secret of her art. She would let no one watch her while she painted, mixed her colors, or prepared her canvases. Secluded as a nun, she stayed in her little room, where a lamp burned perpetually over the mantelpiece before an image of the Mother of God.

Small and withered, with burning dark eyes set in an abnormally pale face, she worked as if in a trance, like some gardener of the mystical, painting the burning bushes behind the holiness of which every temptation lies concealed—fleshy plants bearing fruits fringed with lashes; leaves bearing precious, colorful plumage, eyes peeping out from the riot of their shimmering colors; strange thickets of luscious branches glittering with necklaces of tender berries; and enormous asters from the garden of delights.

Where do they come from, these extraordinary bunches of flowers which seem to have sprouted from her imagination, as though instinctively? Was she inspired by the artificial wreaths used to decorate graves in provincial cemeteries and chapels? Did the cosmic breadth of her vision owe something to the stained-glass windows of the church at Senlis? For, even though Séraphine's paintings are almost compulsive repetitions of

Séraphine Louis: Grapes

stylized leaves and flowers, they are also arabesques of an inner revelation—hieroglyphs that, in the last analysis, could be fully understood only by her and by the God to whom she addressed and dedicated these ecstatic effusions of love.

One day all the light and ardor of her dreams suddenly died. From then on, she went from house to house, preaching the imminent end of the world. Her mind had become vacant and confused. She died in 1934, in a home for the aged at Clermont.

Art was to Séraphine a form of revelation. Painting was a true passion for her, as it had been for Van Gogh. She found release in artistic creation. With eyes wide open she went through the monotonous routine of her dreary life, seeing none of it. Those around her looked upon her as a humble domestic servant. But she had the visionary's gift. She was as though appointed by some higher power to see through the transitory to the eternal. The things of time were to her no more than stage properties: she saw something else, and what she saw she recorded.

Louis Vivin, who worked as an inspector for the French postal services, was unacquainted with the realm of the ecstatic. His only contacts with the mysterious voices of the beyond occurred at spiritualist séances. When he was at his easel he painted the visible world, and he painted it more realistically than it is ever to be seen.

For many years he worked as a mail sorter on French trains. In his rolling post office, he drew up a detailed map of all the postal zones of France, and for this was given a promotion. His other works were conceived in the same spirit, as geographical maps of his intellectual wanderings. His main concern was to set down his recollections. In the twilight of old age, when he had retired and could at last devote himself to his real vocation, he went back over all the streets and squares and bridges where he had walked in the past. He painstakingly went into every detail. He carefully recorded not only groups of houses and bridges as he had seen them but every brick and stone that went into their construction—not only every tree but every leaf of every tree.

Uhde says that Vivin particularly admired Meissonier, especially for his sense of detail. Vivin hated the summary, the generalized. He felt that nothing must be lost when we take inventory of reality, and this discursiveness was an essential characteristic of his art. Everything that exists must be sorted out

and set down for posterity—just as letters in the post office must be sorted and delivered to their destination. Experiences, ideas, perceptions had to be given the stamp of art. He felt that unless he took possession of the world in this way—an approach very close to the bookkeeper's—his experiences would sink into oblivion.

"Whenever I think of Vivin," Uhde writes, "I think of a character in a Maeterlinck play. He is an old man sitting quietly in a lamplit room. Suddenly he becomes aware of inexorable powers surrounding him and his household; and then, without quite realizing it, he correctly interprets the meaning of a strange silence out of doors and the oil lamp's sibilance within the room. Humbled and baffled by the experience, he bows his head, never suspecting that the basic forces of life itself have been his prompters and tutors."

After he retired, Vivin, like St. Jerome in his cell, never left his tiny apartment. Supporting himself on his cane, he painted one image of the world after another, day after day. Often he worked from picture post cards, like Utrillo and the Yugoslav painter Feješ. Quietly and stubbornly, he transformed the things of this world, endowing them with an even more tangible materiality than

they possess: the Trianon, Venice, streets and squares in Paris (colorplate, page 63; page 164). His views always resemble the originals, but Vivin, the architect and builder of cities, has given them his own style. There is real asceticism in the tremulous spidery lines of his pointed brush; with fanatical naïveté, systematically, stone by stone, he rebuilds the Place du Châtelet, the Botanical Garden, Sacré Coeur, Nôtre Dame, the Lion de Belfort, the Moulin de la Galette. The subdued brick red of his walls, the bitter ashen gray of his skies, the blue and black of the Monument to the War Dead, and the desolate colors of the house fronts are truer to life than the originals. This litany of the plainly visible vibrates with the mystery of an indefinable existence.

Why are we held spellbound by these flatly painted, ornamental churches and squares, which he pieced together with such infinite pains and patience? There is no depth in these paintings. Everything is two-dimensional; everything is in the foreground. The people seen in the streets are like dolls in the bluish atmosphere. Vivin shows them to us in frontal view, like the figures in Egyptian tomb portraits. Some other landscape seems to lie behind Vivin's carefully drawn scenes. With childlike clairvoyance, this aging painter created landscapes that obey no laws of matter or perspective, and make no concession to the powers and conventions of style and fashion. Behind the pedantically accurate settings, his world is so true, so naked, so simple, that we give a sigh of relief when we have recognized it.

"Vivin's canvases may seem 'realistic'; every brick and stone, every feature and object, may bespeak a literal intention. But beneath the apparently reportorial surface is a savage sense of tragedy. Louis Vivin was in no respect the Canaletto of modern Paris." (Wilhelm Uhde.)

We might conclude our sketch of Vivin's art with these perspicacious remarks by Wilhelm Uhde. But there is yet another aspect of Vivin's genius: the world that he invented rests upon a structure of pure proportions and pictorial harmonies, whose rhythms and modulations are unconsciously inspired by the spirit of abstraction.

Rousseau, Séraphine, and Vivin were all, in a sense, Uhde's discoveries. Not so Bauchant and Bombois, both of whom he nonetheless knew well as a friend.

Camille Bombois is a folk artist with a strain of unconscious Surrealism. To everything that he paints he communicates some of his own overflowing vitality. Landscapes and objects alike possess their own plastic existence, and the rooms through which he guides us, the bridges that we cross with him, the tree-lined avenues that lead off into the distance, have acquired a depth of their own through his strong lighting, long shadows, and sharp perspective. Human beings are well in the forefront of his interest. Wrestlers, weight lifters, clowns, sword swallowers, fire eaters, gigantic women, both nude and in tights, exhibit and advertise the secrets of human form (colorplate, page 167; page 168). His art conveys the magic of country fairs and circus tents, sideshow freaks, the exciting false glitter of acrobats riding horses to the bittersweet strains of tinny brass bands. Like popular songs, Bombois' art is full of the folklore of the strange and exceptional. His is a colorful peasant fantasy, which has been somewhat affected by the progress of technology, by loudspeakers and player pianos.

His subjects are autobiographical, his scenes those of his own life. Son of a barge owner, Bombois spent his childhood on the canals of the Côte d'Or and of central France. Later, he was a farm laborer, a road worker, an athlete, and a printer. He himself lifted the enormous weights that he depicts for us against a magnificent blue rug (colorplate, page 167). The hero's muscles bulge with their own appreciation of their strength. In the background stands the army of his admirers, all shown in frontal view, their faces frozen in awe at the display of strength.

He began to draw at the age of sixteen and kept on even when he worked as a manual laborer. In 1922 he exhibited his canvases in a Montmartre street. Noël Bureau, a journalist, became enthusiastic about them and wrote an article about him in the little magazine *Rythme et Synthése*. Mathot, an art dealer, was the first to buy his works. Florent Fels and Wilhelm Uhde encouraged him. Bombois had waited a long time for this recognition, confident that it would come, and was now able to devote himself entirely to painting.

He painted as he lived—resolutely, vigorously, but with the delicacy of the physically strong. In his works, everything visible is accurately defined and has been rescued from the uncertainties of light and movement. His outlines are sharp; he has a sober poetic quality that is often reminiscent of cheap color prints and occasionally verges on calendar art. Bombois glories in the heaviness of the weights that he can lift and applies black liberally. He also loves the billiard green of baggy curtains as a frame for the pink legs of his dancers, the velvet reds, the violet yellows, and the tender violets of his circus pictures and brothel interiors. They are in keeping with the massive fleshiness of his rendering of forms (page 168).

He paints in the rude language of athletes and sportsmen, of small-town whores and race-track touts, swaggering, foul-mouthed, and yet possessed with a longing for respectability and an envy of the well-bred.

André Bauchant was a gardener, like his father, and remained one all his life. Even after he took up painting, he still continued to grow fruits and vegetables, which, in his native Touraine, are particularly fine. His mountains, people, and animals all have a vegetable quality; all seem to be sprouting and growing.

During the First World War, Bauchant served in a unit that was sent to the Dardanelles and stationed in Greece. Later, he served in Reims as a telemetric draftsman, and was praised for the accuracy of his work. At the Salon d'Automne of 1921 he exhibited a series of panoramic sketches of the Battle of the Marne, a panoramic view of Châteaurenault, his native town, and a painting

showing the burning of the Temple of the Diana of Ephesus.

He attracted the notice of Le Corbusier, Ozenfant, Lipchitz, and Jeanne Bucher, the art dealer. Sergei Diaghilev commissioned him to design settings for Stravinsky's *Apollon Musagéte*. In 1927 Jeanne Bucher introduced Uhde to the artist, "a tall lean man with a pointed beard, who wore the sort of ill-fitting dark suit that peasants wear to weddings and funerals."

Why did Diaghilev commission Bauchant, who had never seen a ballet nor heard Stravinsky's music, to do the settings? Bauchant's ability to combine the sublimity of the ancient world with a feeling for the contemporary scene at its most ordinary—the mythical with the ironic, a combination which also characterized the *pittura metafisica*—was very much in the spirit of the age.

Without his being aware of it, and without any conscious effort to be so, this was the character of André Bauchant's art. His large-sized historical paintings are peopled with André Bauchant figures disguised as so many Greeks, Romans, or ancient Germans. His *Apotheosis of Homer* of 1927 (page 171) is a good example of this style. In a landscape of gray mountains, we see groups of figures seated, reclining, or standing, dressed in light red-and-orange-colored shirts, reminiscent of old-fashioned bathing suits; in the foreground Homer is chanting the exploits of the Greeks and the Trojans. In the distance, in the clouds high above the mountains, we are given scenes from the *Iliad* and the *Odyssey*. *Neptune* of 1929 (page 170) is similar in conception. Neptune is shown riding the surf—which recalls hair that has been given a permanent wave—as though practicing water skiing. The short-legged god, costumed in red, holds his trident in his right hand, and the reins of his thick-maned horses in his left. He is accompanied by bearded men. In front of him glides a carriage with cupids and gods wearing wigs and costumers' robes, which flap in the breeze. At once ridiculous and magical, this textbook reconstruction of Greek mythology includes some shell motifs.

He also painted *Battle of Thermopylae, Pericles Accounting for the Use of Public Monies, Cleopatra's Barge* (colorplate, page 67), *Capture of the Temple,* and *Adam and Eve* (page 169). In all of these paintings the figures are cottony ghosts painted in fresco-like bright colors of gray or of brown, with childlike fantasy.

What inspired Bauchant to paint these legendary compositions, these scenes of idealized heroes that

André Bauchant: In the Country of Flowers

draw upon the charm of ruins, sun-drenched Alpine landscapes, and secret magic? Unlike Bombois, this painter does not portray his actual experiences; his visions have been borrowed from museums of the imagination, which show the past in a golden glow. They reflect antiquarian knowledge mixed with nineteenth-century conventionalization of tradition, plush exoticism, and Latin bombast. No merely wayward taste, but innocent pleasure in the making of fables has created these family portraits in historical costumes. The scene of one of these classical morality plays no matter where it is supposed to be set, is always painted as his native Touraine, and the ancient heroes are the middle-class inhabitants of his native town.

Bauchant's historical compositions were followed by the works of his late period—flowers (colorplate, page 69), birds, scenes of peasant life, and landscapes. In dull, velvety colors he painted the life of the countryside transfigured in dreams. This Antaeus of painting, who grew fruits and vegetables for a living, delights us with flowers that never grew anywhere save in the fertile soil of a naïve imagination.

The five painters discussed so far were exhibited together for the first time at the Galerie des Quatre Chemins in Paris in 1928. Wilhelm Uhde, who organized the exhibition, called them the "Painters of the Sacred Heart," and taught me, among many others, to understand and "see" them. Some years later, when we had some conversations about the modern primitives, he no longer used this term, which now seemed to him too sentimental. His admiration for the naïve painters no longer stressed the innocence of their personalities so much as the artistic value of their works. I have used his old term in the title of this chapter in tribute to Wilhelm Uhde, a sensitive man and a great art lover, who, although a native of Germany, loved and understood the folk soul of France and its naïve interpreters.

Since then other primitive artists have emerged, in France and in many other countries. The original "Five" had, in a sense, paved the way for them.

In France, a country unusually rich in traditions, where modern primitive art was first discovered, Anatole Jakovsky succeeded Wilhelm Uhde as its sponsor and publicist. The exhibitions that he has organized and his writings on this subject have kept public interest lively and encouraged new talents.

Dominique-Paul Peyronnet, a printer in the town of Talence near Bordeaux, was a poet of the commonplace. He painted landscapes as frozen in dreams—seascapes, woods, views of rivers—and half-dressed women. He defines everything with razor-like sharpness. The waves of the sea are magically motionless, as though made of cut glass, and the ferns and other foliage of the woods he paints are as distinct in individual detail as pearls in a necklace. Peyronnet believed that nature and the human drama should be reproduced with the same precision and fidelity he had learned from the printing of color reproductions. Only about thirty paintings by him are known. *Reclining Woman* (colorplate, page 73) shows a figure in a pink slip and gray silk stockings lying on a dark red couch. Her wavy hair and rather set features suggest erotic tension. There is a little dog in front of the couch, and a pair of women's slippers on the rug. As in the work of Morris Hirshfield, such objects serve as symbols of seductive femininity. It is interesting to note that the walls and the floor are made in part of actual samples of wallpaper pasted on the canvas.

Dominique Lagru, who worked as a shepherd and a miner, is one of the oldest of living naïve painters. He took up painting at seventy-six, and has portrayed an extraordinary menagerie of prehistoric reptiles (page 173). From the museums of natural history and old textbooks on zoology they have emerged and come together in a landscape of tangled olive-green vegetation at the foot of a light-violet mountain covered with tiny palm trees. Picturesque in form and gay in color, they are energetically strangling, killing, and eating one another.

Lagru has conjured up the landscapes and the animals alike from the books that he read in the course of educating himself, rather than from the depths of his imagination. In this, he is like the Polish painter Ociepka. His trees are firmly rooted in real earth, and the branches swaying in the storm, as well as the leaves and flowers painted in innumerable tiny brush strokes, belong to the realm of the painter's waking dreams.

Jules Lefranc was born in Laval, birthplace of the Douanier Rousseau, where he kept a hardware store. He transmuted the ordinary metal objects he handled daily into poetry of the kind that we find in Séraphine's fantastic bouquets. Occasionally, his emphasis upon mechanical things and machine rhythms—for example, blinking signal lights—reminds us of Fernand Léger more than of the Douanier Rousseau. Unlike Léger, however, he did not tame the mechanical aspects of the world into material for still lifes. Rather, he aimed at a mechanical panopticon of the things themselves. His *Railroad Tracks with Eiffel Tower* (page 174), in which wires run parallel high above the streets, with the steel puppet of the Eiffel Tower dancing coquettishly in the background, is a work that already has a classic quality.

Ship's Propellers (Sur le plateau—atelier de la radiale), like the Eiffel Tower picture, is one of a series celebrating ports, factories, machines, and the urban industrial scene in general (page 175). The enormous rust-red hull of a ship extends diagonally across this painting; a little man hoisted by a crane works on the propeller, which looks like an enormous steel bird, with a welding torch. In the distance, a lighthouse, a ship, and a wharf serve as pictorial ornamentation. Lefranc transmutes cubic and cylindrical elements of the machine age into static, illusionistic genre pictures. The painter's naïveté breathes new life into an outmoded romantic style.

Dating from a later period are some landscapes with glowing sunsets and fantastic architecture involving little towers and balconies. Such works as *Pornic, le château* and *Artist's House* (detail, page 174) disclose an undiminished love of precision. The corrosive green of the trees, the poisonous blue of the river, the transparent blue of the sky, and the red-brown of the roofs and flowerpots evoke the lurid colors of a modern country fair.

Emile Blondel, a native of Le Havre, who as a sailor visited many a distant land, later worked as a bus driver in Paris on the J line, which runs from the Place Saint-Michel to the Porte de Clignancourt. He used a pointed brush and hard colors to paint syntheses of the recollections of his travels, both near and far. They are as meticulously rendered as medieval miniatures. These works tell us the story of his childhood and years of wandering, of the cities he saw and the life he observed in them. Anatole Jakovsky says that *Picture of My Life* (page 172) contains more than meets the eye, that hidden and forgotten moods can be sensed in addition to the visible elements.

Blondel's luminous color transforms the dome of the Sacré Cœur and the streets of Montmartre into structures as exotic as anything to be seen in the Orient: the sharp blue of the sky and the jarring note of the green trees are harmonized by means of colorful human figures. Blondel's *Grotto by the Sea*, with figures of people leaving and people left behind

Dominique-Paul Peyronnet: Reclining Woman

on the shore, is no doubt nostalgic of many farewells, a poignant colorprint at once gaily imaginative and faithful to things seen.

Louis Augustin Déchelette, a native of Cours (Rhône), where he worked as a house painter, produced naïve pictures of indignation and protest during the German occupation of France in the Second World War. He had to hide them carefully at the time. They did not see the light of day until Déchelette had gone on to paint a relatively freer and more cheerful world. One of his pictures, *Synthesis of Happiness*, depicts modern man's modes of enjoying himself. The setting is a river bank; we see sports enthusiasts in boats and on motorcycles, children riding ponies and eating ice cream, lovers embracing, and an old man taking refuge in a glass of brandy.

A picture showing a Sunday scene in a village of Beaujolais, *Outdoor Circus* (page 176), and the composition *L'Union des Cœurs* express nothing but joy in living. Déchelette employs soft tones of gray to construct a glowingly decorative world in which jugglers and acrobats, accompanying a wedding procession on its way to the church, celebrate the festive character of life.

As Utrillo painted Montmartre where he lived, so René Rimbert painted his own quarter, that of Saint-Germain des Prés. Rimbert's vision stresses the intensity of perceptions, their forcefulness and clarity, so that we are made aware of the life of the things themselves in the infinite stillness of light, as in the paintings of Jan Vermeer. Although Rimbert has never attained the inwardness or the spiritual control of the Delft master, his pictures convey something of Vermeer's musicality and clarity. The poet Max Jacob, who was a friend of Rimbert, writes that his landscapes reflect the peace of nature and that his trees share the earth's tranquillity.

Few painters have been able to transmute the shabbiness of crumbling walls into such sensitive harmonies of color and form. The grandiose simplicity and austerity of Rimbert's buildings bespeak reflection and contemplation. His carefully observed human figures are shown alone or in groups, standing in dark doorways or walking away down the street. Often they are half obscured by some architectural detail and occasionally cut off by the picture frame. His meditative intensity suggests that something is going on behind the fronts of the houses he paints (page 178).

Like Vivin, Rimbert was a post-office clerk.

Whether he is simple and spontaneous enough to be counted among the naïve painters is an open question; in any case, he is one of the authentic painters of our epoch.

Jean Eve has worked as a miner, railroad man, bookkeeper in a foundry, mechanic, and customs agent. During his travels, he lingered along the banks of France's rivers and recorded these landscapes in an old-fashioned representational manner. In 1924 he saw paintings by Courbet for the first time and was deeply impressed by this artist's realism and vital closeness to nature.

Eve's views of countrysides and cities have a meditative and intimate quality, for all his precise technique and almost photographic naturalism. He paints patchwork fields of golden grain with red-brown and gray-blue roofs, set among trees of delicate green. He also paints bouquets of flowers in subdued colors. Eve has studied art and learned a great deal from professional painters, not without losing some of his original spontaneity.

The Paris-born Jean Fous, after traveling a great deal, eventually settled at the Paris Flea Market, where he has earned a living selling trinkets, postcards, picture frames, and, since 1944, his own paintings.

Some of his works depict scenes from the Flea Market (pages 182, 183); others, the magic of city streets, the malice and humor of metropolitan life. We see people hurrying across a busy intersection, or waiting for customers to turn up or for the weather to change. The events he depicts of life in the Flea Market are permeated with the aroma of futility and transience. The artist seems to suggest, with bitter humor, that in reality, behind this graphically rendered, picturesque animation, the little man is robbed of his life.

Gertrude MacBrady, known as O'Brady, was born in Chicago in 1903 and began to paint in Paris in 1941. Stephen Spender says somewhere that life must break a man before he can write about it. O'Brady's art is her victory over an aimless life: she is engaged in the laborious work of recovering the past, in order to reinvent it—for it is not only the future that may be created, but the past also. *Washerwomen's Boat in the Seine* (page 179) looks back to the turn of the century. It shows a boat with washerwomen, the gently sloping lawns of a park, and ladies in large hats and stiffly ironed dresses, rigid and conventional, looking on while the laundrywomen work. The wash hung up to dry flutters in the wind. On the other side of the river we see factory chimneys and trees in autumnal hues in the gentle light of afternoon; in the foreground a tree stretches over the boat; reflections of the sun play on the long bare branches.

A la bonne Galette (pages 180, 181) was painted in 1941, shortly before the Germans occupied the whole of France and the artist was sent to a concentration camp. The restaurant with the windmill on top of the hill has served as inspiration to many a modern painter. A merry-go-round, painted vivid red, is turning in the green garden. Couples in *fin de siècle* costumes are walking along the gravel paths. A carriage drawn by a white horse rolls by. A lady in a violet dress holds the reins with great elegance and listens to the gentleman in a silk hat beside her. There are also young ladies on swings, a man selling pastry, and the inevitable chef with his high white cap. Here is a slice of life from the past, as though carefully preserved under glass and captured in all its charm, with the careless line and impudent color of the self-taught artist. This is a tribute to an irretrievable bygone era, a rediscovery of the past, not without a touch of melancholy in its nostalgia.

André Demonchy, born in Paris in 1914, is regarded as the youngest of the French naïve painters. He favors rustic scenes and the theme of the change of seasons. He has a special predilection for snow. He was an engineer's helper on the railroads and painted a series of pictures with motifs drawn from this occupation. In technique, he calls to mind a younger Vivin, but he has not the older painter's careful gradations of color. Where Vivin seeks to penetrate the inside of things, Demonchy sees them from the outside. He constructs the bustling urban scene out of brick walls, human figures, medieval towers, and modern vehicles. The painting reproduced on page 187 shows the black file of a funeral procession against a harsh, snow-covered landscape under an overcast, gray-violet sky. In the catalogue of Demonchy's first exhibition, André Breton wrote: "Spring is on its way, and it is Demonchy who makes the hedgerows sing of it, who gives wings to the railway tracks and color to the strawberries—our friend Demonchy whose eyes are filled with little birds...."

Among the other naïve painters in France we may also mention: André Bouquet, whose scenes of city life are like old yellowed maps (page 177); Aristide Caillaud, whose expressive colors and Cubist simpli-

Aloys Sauter: Hymn to World Peace

fications disclose the influence of modern experiments; Jean Schubnel, who reconstructs the old castles in France with a naïvely romantic imagination; and F. Boilauges (page 186).

Although there is no end to life, there must be to writings about it. We may conclude this chapter on the naïve painters of France with a contemporary artist whose place and date of birth are not known: Aloys Sauter. He lived at Montreil, near Paris, and was a furniture maker. His paintings celebrate the industriousness of the artisan, and world peace.

If there is such a thing as unwitting Surrealism, we may find it in Sauter's works, with their unexpected combinations of objects, all painted with hallucinating intensity, which reveal a poetically naïve fantasy unrealistic in its simplicity. In his *Cabinetmaker's Workshop* (pages 184, 185) the dining-room sideboard stands in the center like a monument. The master himself is shown twice—it is as though we had two stills from a film—first, working with the plane and, second, with the chisel. His wife, who is shown here in a green dress next to a vase of flowers, wrote a poem to the beauty of this piece of furniture, which begins:

Cette merveille
faite à la main
est sans pareille
c'est bien certain...

[This marvel
All handmade
Has no equal
That's quite certain...]

The long poem, which may be read on the scroll at the right-hand side of the picture, ends with the words "Verse of Madame Sauter Catellier, poetess."

Madame Sauter is portrayed again in the painting *Hymn to World Peace* (colorplate, page 79), this time as the central figure. In the compressed landscape of a rose-trellised garden we see stairs and an arched bridge. All the family pets—cats, a dog, and a parrot—have gathered to listen to the poetess's reading of her verses on world peace. She wears a black lace dress, holds her text in a plump right hand, and a red flower in her left. Above her head we see the dove of peace with a branch in its beak. Madame Sauter recites with deep emotion, leaning against the table behind her—a pose employed by singers in the provinces, obviously admired by the artist for its elegance.

In his utter unself-consciousness, the artist is amazingly successful in crossing the line between the atmosphere of the country fair and Promethean dream: the worthiest intentions are mingled with real-life gruesomeness, enchantment with horror. This art is on the frontier between pious banality and Surrealist depth.

Even though the naïve painters fall outside all styles and schools, they nonetheless—particularly in France, the land of incessant artistic metamorphoses—unconsciously reflect the experiments that contemporary professional artists have carried out deliberately and with the greatest intellectual concentration.

These simple, innocent souls fearlessly confronted the things of their world and called them by their real names, without regard for tradition or convention. Out of the sincerity of their belief, they separated what was living from what was dead in the life around them, and occasionally they succeeded in inspiring new myths of everyday life.

... They will wait listening, silent and brooding as the frost, to time, strange ticking time, dark time that haunts us with the briefness of our days. They will think of men long dead, of men now buried in the earth, of frost and silence long ago, of a forgotten face and moment of lost time, and they will think of things they have no words to utter.

Thomas Wolfe, Of time and the River

VII American Primitives from Colonial Times to the Present

The first stirrings of a secular folk art began to be felt in America about three centuries ago, when the common man discovered techniques with which he could express himself despite lack of formal instruction.

This popular art was not produced under the same conditions as that of France, where the naïve painters were occasional eccentrics on the periphery of a highly sophisticated professional art. The naïve painters of America did not appear outside a main current of general development; they shared the ideas and tastes of the early settlers, whose portraits they painted and whose houses they decorated.

The art of the farmers, preachers, artisans, and housewives of America has been all the closer to the spirit of the young and growing nation because, from the first, it has had hardly any tradition to assimilate. Once freed from the European colonial system, the United States burned its bridges to the Old World. The nascent longing for artistic expression found perfectly adequate form in the paintings of amateurs or naïve professionals. This art came into being spontaneously, out of the various needs to report, to entertain, and to earn a living.

In most European countries, "amateur" artists were influenced by the prevalent official styles. Calling themselves *dilettanti*, they painted—with lesser skill and less adequate technique; that is to say, imperfectly—the same subjects as schooled academic painters. On the other hand, the authentic naïve painters of Europe stood apart from the prevailing cultural fashion. They did not imitate official art; they painted the world as they saw and felt it.

In America, especially in the beginning, the contrast between the dilettanti and the naïve painters was not so marked. Many men and women painted to add beauty to their environment, to preserve the features of their loved ones, or to record important private and public events. The folk painters produced portraits, memorials, landscapes, still lifes, genre paintings, and allegorical paintings. Clerics and teachers supplied ornamental decorations for marriage and baptismal certificates; ladies painted arrangements of fruits, flowers, and memorial portraits of the dead. In "young ladies' seminaries," instruction was given in the art of watercolor and of painting on silk and velvet, along with reading, writing, and dancing. In addition to this genteel amateur art, there was a more professional art produced by self-taught artists who executed lifelike portraits, views of farms, and other subjects in accordance with the wishes of those who commissioned them and the amount they were paid. These self-taught naïve artists were mostly artisans—cartwrights, carpenters, house painters, or sign painters—whose occupations made them familiar with the paint medium. They did not practice art as a hobby, but as a source of income. There was no sharp demarcation line as yet between art and handicrafts. The majority of works of the late seventeenth and early eighteenth centuries are unsigned. These folk artists did not study the old masters; they drew upon their own imagination, talent, and craft. They worked on their own; no sovereign, no patrician patron aided them. They lived as the people lived and were supported by those whose vital needs they helped to gratify.

These painters, active from the seventeenth century on, were called "limners"—the term is presumably derived from "illumination." They were anonymous in the same sense as medieval painters. Like other craftsmen of the time, they were engaged in the struggle for survival. They could hardly have suspected that their art would become an object of lively interest a few centuries later.

The limners were itinerant artists. They traveled far and wide, decorating farmers' houses both with pictures that followed stereotyped models and with more freely painted landscapes, murals, and portraits. Occasionally, they spent the winter months readying backgrounds for portraits—painting costumes, jewelry, and often the hands—leaving space for the faces to be added later. For this reason, limners' portraits are often extremely simplified, suggesting types, and all but devoid of individual character. There were portraitists who painted directly from life. but even their portraits, stereotyped in pose and gesture, stiffly drawn in plain, harsh colors, reveal an instinctive search for simplification and schematization.

The primitive American portraitists of the seventeenth and the eighteenth centuries may be compared to the primitive Serbian artists of the Voivodina, active in the eighteenth century, whose portraits, though sensitive, are also of a curious stiffness. They, too, were newcomers to the country in which they found themselves—refugees from the Turkish invasion of the Balkans. In their works appear faint echoes of the Viennese baroque. The American primitives were similarly influenced by Dutch and English traditions. Both in America and in the Voivodina the portraits had a rigid, wooden quality. For all their talent in characterization, and for all their instinctive sense of composition, these artists lacked the courtly elegance, the delicate, sensuous colors, and the classical precision of their models. Nevertheless, these self-taught men succeeded in conveying essential features of their subjects.

In the New England states, as well as in Pennsylvania, New York, and New Jersey, which were centers of trade, industry, and handicrafts, this primitive art was largely practiced in small towns. The larger cities imported art from abroad for their more sophisticated inhabitants.

Down to the middle of the eighteenth century, portrait painting predominated. Landscapes and genre scenes came later, and by the middle of the nineteenth century, historial scenes enjoyed particular favor.

The limners of the second half of the seventeenth century, for all the quality of their works, are known only by the names of their sitters or the subjects of their pictures. The painter, active c. 1670, who portrayed a Mr. and Mrs. Freake with their child, is called the "Freake Limner." The portraitist, active in the same period, of the Mason family, is referred to as the "Mason Limner." The adults and children portrayed here with puritanic austerity and crude naïveté look out at us from that century with the frozen expression of the sitters for daguerreotype photographs in a later day. The portrait of Miss Dennison, painted by an unknown artist c. 1775, belongs to this group, as well as Benjamin Parker's portrait of a little boy holding a watch, painted between 1800 and 1804 (page 189).

For two centuries the limners performed a function very similar to that of portrait photographers. They provided even quite humble people with a gallery of ancestors. These portraits began to come down from the attics where they had been gathering dust when an epoch tired of technology and mechanization rediscovered them.

Joseph H. Davis, who lived at Newfield, Maine, and painted c. 1836, was nicknamed Fine Hill Joe, because every spring he set out on his cross-country wanderings. On these trips he found people willing to pay for a family portrait. His sitters are usually shown in silhouette, their faces in severe profile, and occasionally the works bear the signature "Joseph H. Davis, painted with the left hand." More than one hundred of his watercolors are known today. He probably died during one of his tours.

Joseph Whiting Stock, a contemporary of Davis, was active as a painter in Springfield, Mass. At the age of eleven he had an injury which left his legs paralyzed, so that he was unable to follow a "normal" profession. He advertised his talent in newspapers and obtained many commisions. He painted over a thousand portraits. His poetic likenesses of children, some done in death, are deeply moving in their stiff way. A passage from Thomas Wolfe comes to mind:

"A thousand voices—his father's, his brothers', and of the child that he himself had been, and all the lives and voices of the hundred others, the lost, the vanished people, were whispering to him."

William Matthew Prior was an itinerant portrait painter (page 188). In 1828 he advertised in a newspaper that he could provide a correct likeness of his sitters for $35, frames included. However, anyone satisfied with a flat portrait could obtain one for $10.

Prior died about 1873, thirty years after the physicist Arago had given his paper on Daguerre's photographic process before the Academy of Science in Paris. The advent of photography spelled the end of the limner.

Among the folk artists who painted imaginary scenes, the best known is Edward Hicks. He was born in Attleboro, Pa. (now Bensalem). At the age of thirteen he was apprenticed to a coachmaker; seven years later he opened his own shop. He wandered through many states, preaching at Quaker meetings, and painted in a charmingly archaic, dignified style. One of his favorite subjects is based on the famous text in Isaiah 11:6: "The wolf also shall dwell with the lamb, and the leopard shall lie down with the kid; and the calf and the young lion and the fatling together; and a little child shall lead them." This provided the theme of his many versions of the *Peaceable Kingdom*. One of these shows a chubby child and a number of animals lying peacefully together; in the background, William Penn and his friends are seen making a peace treaty with Indian chieftains, and behind them are a lake with sailboats and a mountain in blue light. At the corners are allegorical compositions with symbolic white lambs and doves of peace.

Hicks favored large-size historical compositions. Among them are *Washington Crossing the Delaware*, dating from 1835, which for a time served as a bridge sign, and *American Declaration of Independence* of 1845. He is particularly successful with his animals, whether allegorical, as in *Noah's Ark* (pages 190, 191), or observed in scenes of farm life. *Cornell Farm*, painted c. 1848 (colorplate, page 87) shows a landscape of softly rolling country and, in the foreground, horses, cows, and pigs. At the right a young colt stands close to its mother. Their beauty and health can be seen and appreciated; each animal is recognizable as an individual, like each face in a group portrait by a minor Dutch master. The viewer keeps discovering new details: little figures wearing stovepipe hats—men conversing, no doubt about the crops or market prices. There are a plowman, a fence, some sheep, houses, barns with red roofs, and many other things.

Jenny Emily Snow's *Belshazzar's Feast* is a religious allegory, evoking both the visible and immanent evidences of God's wrath with naïve fantasy. In the airy spaciousness of a classic architectural setting, the Biblical scene of terror is evoked with the vividness of nightmare. The figures wear fanciful modern costumes, as though the whole thing were taking place at the Paris Opéra. It may be mentioned here that the works of the naïve painters of America often reflect the intense religious life of their country.

Next in popularity to historical paintings and religious compositions were scenes from daily life, depicting men at work or leisure. From Linton Park to Grandma Moses, a continuous line of artists has treated the life of the farmer and the patriarchal community of the village.

Linton Park's *Flax Scutching*, dating from about 1860 (pages 192, 193) depicts the collective activities of the village population with realistic humor and robustness. The artist has combined the portrayal of men at work with comical scenes to achieve a vivid genre painting; a gently lyrical landscape provides the background.

Thomas Chambers painted romantic views of the Hudson, waterfalls on the Genesee, and dramatic views of Niagara Falls. One of these shows a solitary figure standing on a rock, looking at the rapids and at the iridescent curtain that is formed by drops of mist and shimmers like powdered glass. Chambers was active between 1835 and 1853 in the state of New York. After 1853 his name disappeared from the records.

About 1840, R. Costa, who is said to have been a ship's cook before taking up art, painted on wood panels his small, very primitive pictures portraying the life of the whaler. These paintings bring to mind Melville's famous tale of the "all-destroying but never defeated whale."

Joseph Pickett was a carpenter. As a young man, he traveled with a circus. In summer, he occasionally operated shooting galleries at country fairs, decorated with his own pictures. After he married, he opened a grocery store, and in his spare time painted in the back room. He ground his own colors from berries that he picked in the woods, and made his own brushes by drawing cats' hairs through a quill pen. Since he worked over his paintings for months, occasionally for years, his output was small. The few discovered so far date from the last years of his life. They were put up for auction when he died in 1918, and were sold for a dollar apiece.

Edward Hicks: Cornell Farm

He painted *Coryell's Ferry, 1776, and Washington Taking Views* (colorplate, page 194). It is a summer landscape he had visited, but he chose to imagine how it would have looked more than a century earlier. There is a little stream, a tiny millhouse with water wheel, and neat little farmhouses nearby. The latter are so frankly spick-and-span that we can only wonder what life goes on within them. The woods above are done with heavy brushwork, and we just make out the figure of George Washington in eighteenth-century clothes, observing the scene with a spyglass. A red deer casts its shadow in the water; three ducks are swimming in perfect alignment; the white horse stands meekly near the water mill, waiting for its master to come back (page 195). As is not unusual with self-taught painters, the artist has here attempted to give a more realistic impression by pasting material of mosslike texture on the picture; also the white ripple of the waves is illusionistically enhanced with spots of plaster. As in Oriental miniatures the various parts of the picture are placed one above the other in a single plane. For all the meticulous treatment of details, the composition as a whole is a poetic vision of the transience and permanence of a landscape.

Pickett's well-known painting *Manchester Valley* was bought for one dollar by his widow at the auction held after his death. She gave it to the local school (shown in the painting), but later the school sold this landscape, which had in the interval become a valuable possession, to finance the building of a new schoolhouse. The toylike train seen moving across the landscape is supposed to depict the first train that passed through New Hope, Pa., the painter's birthplace.

Joseph Becker painted the first train passing through the snowy landscape of the Sierra Nevada (page 196) with refreshing candor. We see Chinese and American workers who have come in their snowshoes to watch the event, the smoking engine, the red wheels, the yellow coaches, doll-like human figures, and high snow-covered mountains. The organization is graphic, the colors childlike and graceful. The smoke is gray on the white snow, and we can almost hear the tooting of the engine.

The artistic quality of many of these painters may seem inadequate when their fantasy fails to keep pace with native vigor and to integrate the meticulously observed details into a self-contained whole. Even so, these naïvely painted anecdotes provide a poetic glimpse into the social and psychological life of the American continent (pages 198, 199). Occasionally a painter is known only by a single work, and yet has therein expressed something unique and memorable. H.M.T. Powell painted the blacksmith J.M. Studebaker in his smithy. The three men with bellows and anvil are figures of legend; we have the impression that the black-bearded master Studebaker in his silk hat has gathered with his apprentices in their odd headgear to sing a sad song predicting the impending revolution which will make all such craft enterprises obsolete.

Toward the middle of the nineteenth century, two artists, almost simultaneously, treated two characteristically American subjects—Negro music and boxing. D. Morrill painted his *Banjo Player* (page 197) about 1860. The picture shows a young Negro with his hat pushed jauntily to the back of his head. His skin is dark, his fuzzy hair is black, and his legs in striped red and brown trousers against the pale green wall are tapping out a light-footed dance step. The moon-shaped banjo glistens as it plunks out the rhythms of the jazz-mad America that was to come. George A. Hayes painted one of the first pictures of sportsmen (colorplate, page 201; page 200), entitled

With Bare Fists. Inside the ring we see the boxers stripped to the waist, wearing fancy tights and white stockings; the referees stand in a ring outside the prize ring, and the public crowds around behind them. Three of the fighters wear brown tights and three wear red tights. Painstaking care has gone into the rendering of detail, and great excitement is conveyed, for all that the figures are frozen in attitudes of immobility.

In 1870, S. F. Milton painted the funeral of Abraham Lincoln. The black horses with their black plumes fluttering move slow-gaitedly to a funeral march as the President is taken to his grave. Officers carrying long swords accompany the solemn procession. The naïve painters of America have repeatedly taken the Great Emancipator for subject, retelling the legend of his life and death in the solemn, literal manner of the history books. In the background a gray mass of soldiers with rifles stands at attention, forming a wall. No human face is to be seen; the picture is of a formal ritual that covers over the terror of death with the properties of convention.

Another picture of a popular hero's end is *John Brown on the Way to Execution* (colorplate, page 203;

89

page 202), by the Negro painter Horace Pippin. Brown, a farmer, land surveyor, and pastor was a foe of slavery, but his struggle against it was premature. In October, 1859, with eighteen of his men, he stormed the arsenal at Harpers Ferry in Virginia. This was to be the signal for a general uprising of the slaves. Deeply moved by this martyr's death, Pippin painted John Brown being taken to the place of execution. His painting has itself the quality of a popular ballad, recalling the Northern song of the Civil War:

John Brown's body lies a-moldering in the grave,
His soul is marching on . . .

The group on the wagon is clearly outlined against the background of chalk-white houses. John Brown wears a broad-rimmed hat, as do the guards who accompany him. Like the early Christian painters, modern naïve painters often identify their heroes by specific attributes: here John Brown is identified only by the rope around him. His friends stand in silence, facing the wagon. It is December; they are bundled up in cloaks and scarves. The figures at the right turn their faces to the viewer. Don't they know what is taking place?

This is the language of poetry, with the simplicity, candor, and naïveté that characterize all authentic popular art. Albert C. Barnes called this painting distinctively American. Its dramatic vividness, crudity, simplicity, picturesqueness, and accentuated rhythms find their musical parallel in the Negro spirituals.

Horace Pippin began to paint religious pictures at the early age of ten. He was fifteen when he left school. He worked unloading coal at a coal yard, then got a job as a porter in a hotel. Later he was employed in a foundry, and he also peddled old clothes. During the First World War he fought in France and was severely wounded. Back in America, he painted a large number of works until his death in 1947: scenes from the life of Negroes, landscapes, war recollections, religious motifs, and still lifes. In his autobiographical notes, he says: "My opinion of art is that a man should have love for it, because my idea is that he paints from his heart and mind. To me it seems impossible for another to teach one of Art."

One of the most important recent American primitives was John Kane. Born near Edinburgh in 1860, he went to America at the age of nineteen and settled in Pittsburgh. He worked as a miner, carpenter, and steelworker, and toward the end of his life as a house painter. "I began painting steel cars," Kane writes, "and in this way I learned the use of paint." In 1927 the Carnegie International Exhibition in Pittsburgh accepted his paintings. Kane was the first primitive to be recognized in the United States. His art brought him little in the way of material rewards: he died a poor man, of tuberculosis, in 1934.

Kane painted portraits, interiors, and scenes of public celebration, but above all the visual aspects of Pittsburgh where he lived—its smoke-blackened factories where he himself had worked, its gloomy cobblestone streets, and its peculiar architectural marriage of classicist façades with concrete skyscrapers and steel bridges. One of his best-known paintings is *Touching Up* (page 205), which portrays the painter in his studio. He worked with great patience and precision. Thanks to his strong sense of composition, he could incorporate a great many details in a picture without destroying its unity. His well-known *Self-portrait* (page 204) expresses intense concentration. With utmost truthfulness he depicts his aging body and the austere dignity of his spirit. The curves, ellipses, and angles upon which his works are built bring to mind the ritual formulas

of icon painting. We might detect in this portrait a distant echo of the period when he was a prize fighter—man depicted as struggling alone in the prize ring of the universe. The question of the meaning of man's existence is asked here with candor, directness, and force.

One of the most interesting recent primitives is Morris Hirshfield, who at the age of sixty-five began to paint fantastic animals with closely woven textures reminiscent of Persian miniatures, and female nudes contemplating their mirrored images in transparently erotic dreams.

Hirshfield was born in a small town in Russian Poland in 1872. At the age of eighteen he emigrated to the United States. He found a job in a women's coat factory, and later became a manufacturer of boudoir slippers. In 1937, following a severe illness, he retired from his business, and from then on he devoted himself entirely to painting.

His experience as a tailor seems to have left a lasting imprint on his style: landscapes, human figures, and animal figures, all seem to have been cut out from patterns. But behind these naïve forms there vibrates an unrealistically troubling, challengingly absurd something—a soul unburdens its private dreams in hypnotic surrender to sensuous color and linear form (page 208).

His works were publicly shown for the first time in 1943, at the Museum of Modern Art in New York, in an exhibition arranged by Sidney Janis, the American critic and collector of primitive art.

Hirshfield's *Tiger* (page 206) dates from 1940. His model was a colored illustration that he had found in a children's book. But he transmuted the banal original into a mythical beast with tiny feet and hypnotic eyes, endowing it with a compelling, magical vitality. *Girl Before the Mirror* (colorplate, page 93) was the first nude that he dared to paint. From shyness, he painted a back view—and even the mirrored image is a back view, in contradiction to the laws of optics. His tiger seems to be wearing a well-tailored striped man's suit, and the nude girl, whose image is shown twice (in front of the mirror and in it), brings to mind the folded-over cloth used to make the back of a garment. Hirshfield's lion—shown walking in a garden and carefully avoiding the flowers—wears a well-kept fur coat with a magnificent fur collar.

Sidney Janis tells us of the shock that he received the first time that he saw *Angora Cat*, when the two round eyes of the animal, gleaming in the darkness, returned his stare. This, he says, reminded him of the sequence in the film *Duck Soup*, when Groucho Marx comes upon an unexpected image in his mirror and is taken aback, only to find the image, oddly enough, immobile. Such were the luminous eyes of Hirshfield's cat, this strangely compelling creature sitting on a couch in a very feminine pose.

Hirshfield usually starts a picture by making an outline drawing of his subject. He applies his paint impulsively, as inspiration dictates. To render the texture of the lion's mane as realistically as possible, he used a comb to work out individual strands. These gentle, erotic, domesticated, yet still dangerous beasts from children's books and his own imagination convey something of the ecstatic visions of a childhood in eastern Europe (page 207). But the feverish dreams are controlled and have been poetically condensed: each of his figures is a representative symbol of his inner world, an image of power, possession, fear, or temptation.

Nude with Flowers (page 209) shows a woman against a dark background patterned with small branches. She holds a flowering bush in one hand; a bird is perched on one finger of the other. Her breasts and pelvis are covered with flowers, and she is surrounded with colorful birds of paradise. A more de-

lightfully naïve expression of wish fulfillment could hardly be imagined.

Patrick J. Sullivan, painter of the super-real, interpreter of symbolic landscapes, and preacher of allegorical intellectual systems, goes beyond the rational in search of unknown dimensions of experience. He uses a simple technique to express his candid philosophical meditations. His dreams and symbols are often gloomy; but their gruesomeness sometimes has the unintended comical quality of *grand guignol.*

In 1936 Sullivan painted a work that he titled *Man's Procrastinating Pastime.* In the secret fastnesses of a forest, man is burying the evil part of himself. He does this secretly, with a bad conscience, like a murderer trying to destroy the evidence of his crime. The good part of man is standing by, urging the other to come back into the light of day and perform good deeds. To the right of the standing figure is a grotesque personification of sin, a creature with large awkward feet and bony hands. The other elements of the picture, e. g., the trees, are also intended as symbols.

A year later, Sullivan painted *An Historical Event,* depicting the romance of Edward VIII and Mrs.

Wallis Simpson. This work recalls the rich popular literature of the time which celebrated the triumph of love over all obstacles, and is akin in spirit to the calypsos composed by West Indian singers on the same occasion. Sullivan introduced all sorts of ideas into his no less sentimental ballad on eternal love. The trees stand in perfect alignment, recalling the fur-capped sentries in front of Buckingham Palace. The face on the British lion—he is about to walk out of the picture to symbolize the act of abdication —resembles Edward more than the face on the Edward figure kneeling in front of Mrs. Wallis Simpson, who is portrayed as a flower.

The Fourth Dimension (page 210), which dates from 1938, is even more philosophical and original in conception. Man, "a three-dimensional creature," as the artist put it, is seen chained to the three-dimensional planet and looking out upon the infinite universe, in which worlds and planets soar like gleaming balloons. Alone and helpless in the face of passing time (symbolized by an hourglass), he tries in vain to decipher the infinite. However, death (reclining figure) breaks the chain that is holding man to earth, and his spirit (a female figure) soars into the infinite, transcending all physical limitations. "It is impossible to show the fourth dimension ob-jectively," says Sullivan. "I just call it Sullivan's Universe."

Sullivan was born at Braddock, Pa., in 1894. His father, a farmer, died leaving five children, and Patrick grew up in an orphanage. At fifteen he got a job in a printing plant; it was at this time that he made his first attempts to paint. Later he worked as assistant manager of municipal playgrounds in Wheeling, W. Va., and again tried to paint. This activity was interrupted by the war. He served as an instructor in training camps and eventually became a master sergeant in the regular army. Not until 1919, when he secured a job with American Railway Express, did he begin seriously to paint. "I never took an art lesson in my life," he says. "I just like to paint and from now on I shall paint things that come to mind—powerful stuff that will make people think—that's my goal."

The literary—and most prominent—aspect of Sullivan's art suggests an eccentric who broods on the fate of man and the world, with the philosophy of a self-taught man. But a mysterious landscape leads a ghostlike existence behind his narratives— a landscape with its own pictorial logic. His intellectually immature world is filled with human drama.

Theora Hamblett, who was born in Mississippi in 1895 and still lives there, is also given to philosophical meditations. One of her paintings is entitled *Vision* (page 210). Signs appear in a cloud, repeated four times. A man in yellow clothes stands in front of a wood and looks at the sky. The circular white cloud hovers above the trees in the dark-blue night sky. In the second part of the picture—which is like the first except for being lighter—a yellow sign resembling a grid makes its appearance; this yellow sign is also seen in the third and fourth parts. Does the sign stand for the gateway to Paradise? for the Heavenly Jerusalem? or is it a closed door? The man who looks at it does not change his position throughout the four visions. The windows and door of his house have a yellow glow. At his left is a little pine tree. One of his hands is raised to shield his eyes from the brilliance of the apparition.

Unlike Hirshfield, who draws upon unconscious psychological sources, and unlike Sullivan, who draws upon the domain of metaphysics, Anna Mary Robertson Moses, better known as Grandma Moses, takes her inspiration exclusively from the realm of the visible. She depicts the everyday world of a farmer's existence, idealizing it in retrospect; her art is one of lingering reflection, a survey of and final tribute to a full life that has now run its course. In her work, that forgotten past acquires great vividness; and the permanence of the land and the life sprouting from it is emphasized. With the farsightedness of old age she goes back to the events of her childhood—days of work and days of play—to the period when she raised her own family, and to the occasions when she went away from home. For instance, she paints a Christmas homecoming which brings friends and family from far and near (page 243); a parlor spotlessly clean for Sunday; or the steamy atmosphere of washday. She paints the fragrance and colors of freshly plowed earth, the thousand greens of Cambridge Valley in the state of New York, with its meadows, woods, hills, lilac-colored skies, and roads glistening in the snow with the delicate gray tracks of old-fashioned sleighs.

"When I paint, I study and study the outside lots of times," Grandma Moses writes in her autobiography. "Often I get at a loss to know just what shade of green I should take, and there are a hundred trees that have each three or four shades of green in them. I look at a tree and I see the limbs, and then the next part of the tree is a dark, dark black green, then I have got to make a little lighter green, and so on. And then on the outside it'll either be a yellow green or whitish green, that's the way the trees are shaded. And the snow—they tell me I should shade it more or use more blue, but I have looked at the snow and looked at the snow, and I can see no blue; sometimes there is a little shadow, like the shadow of a tree, but that would be gray instead of blue, as I see it."

Grandma Moses' lovely winter landscapes have occasionally been compared to Brueghel's winter paintings. But where the Flemish master composes broad rhythmic harmonies of color and space, Grandma Moses meticulously and candidly enumerates the data of her everyday world. Trusting her sense of the decorative, she inserts figures or scenes wherever an empty spot seems to require them. For this reason she should rather be compared to the medieval illuminators, who filled the pages of calendars and Books of Hours with scenes of human activities.

The serenity of old age reflected in Grandma Moses' works is not of itself sufficient to account for their appeal. To transmute one's experiences into a joyful affirmation of life also presupposes a native gift of expression. Grandma Moses possesses that gift to a high degree. She picks out the best of her memories and shares them with us, with the friendly smile characteristic of her country (page 212). "What's the use of painting a picture if it isn't something nice?" she writes. "So I think real hard till I think of something pretty, and then I paint it. I like to paint old-timey things, historical landmarks of long ago, bridges, mills, and hostelries, those old time homes, there are a few left, and they are going fast. I do them all from memory, most of them are day dreams, as it were. . . ."

Israel Litwak has preserved the innocence of a child's vision. His landscapes and people are directly experienced and expressed with genuine spontaneity. His summer and winter scenes are peopled with grotesque creatures. He renders the atmosphere of a winter day, the dull blue of a frozen pond surrounded by the coral-like branches of trees covered with rime (page 215). He began to paint at seventy, when he could no longer work at his regular occupation of cabinetmaking. He said that if he ever stopped working he would die; and so he paints.

Lawrence Lebduska, a stained-glass worker born in Baltimore and educated in Europe, has created detailed landscapes filled with human and animal figures. His style is halfway between the folklore tradition and a spontaneous interpretation of reality (page 215).

Thorvald Arenst Hoyer, a former acrobat, organizes his pictorial world with an outspoken predilection for contrasts. He composes his luminous spots of color into geometric fields, artificial flowers, and leaf ornaments. The result is landscapes and interiors painted in a naïve pointillist manner (colorplate, page 99).

Clara Williamson grew up on the Texas frontier among cowboys, wild horses, and herds of cattle. Her schematized paintings of longhorn cattle are reminiscent of Egyptian hunting scenes or the frescoes of Tassili.

Emile White depicts man's solitude in the overpopulated big cities of this century. With the artlessness of a folk song he expresses man's homelessness in the stony jungles of civilization. With Thomas Wolfe, he seems to be saying that man is exiled and alone. In one of the two works reproduced here (page 214), a man is seen sitting on a black suitcase in the middle of the sidewalk, waiting for whatever is to come. The other shows a large crowd marching behind a banner with an inscription paraphrasing the old slogan of the oppressed, "Strangers of the world unite! You have nothing to lose but your loneliness."

Pedro Cervantez, who was born in Arizona, works for the Santa Fe Railway, and is a naïve interpreter of the beauty of technology. He loves the geometric order and the repetitions that characterize mechanical constructions. A croquet ground, for all the realism with which its hard shadows and linear structures are rendered, becomes an abstract painting. Both *Panhandle Lumber Company*, with the grid of parallel fence posts and the wires of the railway signal, and *Cuates Privadas*, showing a privy in a desert landscape, the washing on the line flapping in the wind, are intensely primitive echoes of the artist's vision of modern technology.

Samuel Koch came to New York from Warsaw in 1910. For several years he ran a small store; later he was a milliner, and in his spare time painted such subjects as bouquets of artificial flowers on a red table, people alone in the atmosphere of the big city, and religious gatherings of humble men whose mask-like features reflect hope for the Messiah's coming.

Streeter Blair was a waiter, a drummer in a theater orchestra, a traveling salesman for a textile firm, a principal of a school, and an antique dealer. He has painted scenes from all these periods of his life, such as *Christmas Tree Market in Los Angeles*, with farmers and bankers discussing money matters. *Outing in 1840* (page 211) shows an old-fashioned train chugging off to the left and a horse-drawn carriage passing in the street against a background of bare houses. *Band Concert in Kansas, 1911* shows the inhabitants of a small town gathered around the little pavilion, watching the players merrily making music. The whole town seems to have gathered for the summer night's entertainment: little pig-tailed girls flanked by mother and father, infants in arms, eaters of ice cream and melons, laborers in shirt sleeves, well-dressed couples, boys standing on their heads, elegant horse-drawn carriages. In the background a friendly moon is rising, and in the distance the sun is setting.

In 1938 the Museum of Modern Art in New York held the first large exhibition of European and American "popular painting." Since then, art historians and collectors have displayed a lively interest in this art. Frequent exhibitions have acquainted the public with it, and many works were moved from local collections to larger museums. There is no doubt that the modest efforts of the naïve painters have exerted some influence on their "colleagues," the professional artists. As the most important North American naïve painters of this century, we might single out Joseph Pickett, John Kane, and Morris Hirshfield. Or is it still too early to say which of the many refreshing works by modern primitives will prove of permanent value?

A naïve art nourished from different sources came into being in Central and South America and the islands of the Caribbean.

The small island of Hispaniola (Haiti and the Dominican Republic) in the Caribbean was discovered by Columbus, who named it La Española. The gold mines discovered there by subsequent travelers were at first exploited with the help of the Indian natives. These were later replaced with Caribs from the Bahamas, and finally with Negro slaves brought from Africa. Spanish, French, and English cultural influences combined here with archaic and primitive

Thorwald Arenst Hoyer: Inside a Barn

currents—and Catholic ritual with the secret voodoo cults, African fetishism, and the waning myths of the ancient Indian religion.

Not the island itself, but its peculiar cultural mixture and the artistic sensibility of its inhabitants were rediscovered by De Witt Peters, an American, in 1943. He was sent to Haiti from the United States to teach English. After six months he resigned from his teaching post. Having discovered the naïve painters of Haiti, he devoted himself full time to their artistic development. In 1945 he founded an art center at Port-au-Prince which encouraged young talents and organized exhibitions.

One of Peters' discoveries was the voodoo priest Hector Hyppolite, painter of mysterious rites and incantations (page 219). Carvers of fetishes and painters of animistic pictures are to be found outside as well as inside Haiti, but, in most other places, the gods and demons have lost their magic powers from contact with modern civilization, and images of them are sold to tourists as souvenirs. Hyppolite's demons are different. He spent his youth traveling in America and Africa. He saw both the old and the new powers of life with the eyes of a man at once primitive and civilized, and his paintings convey something of the mentality of tribal Negroes converted to Christianity. His suggestive imagery has probably influenced the Cuban Surrealist painter Wifredo Lam, and the poet André Breton has devoted essays to his art.

The magical paintings of Enguérrand Gourgue, related to those of Hyppolite, combine elements derived from pre-Christian cults, folklore, and the modern approach to the object. *Magic Table* (page 217) dates from 1947 and shows devils, magic symbols, and children's masks. On a table we see a snake coiled around a horse's head. The horse's head is horned, and flashes of lightning come from its eyes; next to it are candles and a small devil-figure. Two winged demons are in the doorway; one is carrying a naked human figure, the other a torch pointed downward. A transparent cubic receptacle attached to the wall (or is it a niche?) contains feet and hands—perhaps sacrificial offerings. The work evokes an alien sphere of life and imagination—evil visions in yellow, brown, and black. Many of the objects seem to come directly from the fantastic world of Surrealism. The demonism is, at the same time, both clumsy and naïve; it suggests a performance of magic deliberately calculated to inspire shudders.

The colors are luminous and follow a calculated rhythmic order.

Next to Hyppolite, it is above all Philomé Obin who gathers the young talents of Haiti around him. Obin was successively a civil servant, a barber, a coffee salesman, and a house painter. He treats scenes of popular life from the past and the present with naïve realism. *The Burial of Charlemagne Peralta* evokes the gloomy splendor surrounding the death of a powerful leader. A procession of soldiers, priests, and followers moves through streets lined with people. The picture is accurate in detail and rigorous in order; at the same time it expresses grief. The drawing is rather summary, but the coloring is very sensitive. A painting of a fisherman conveys the loneliness of a man who lives face to face with featureless expanses of water.

A motif that Haitian painters have treated with many variations is the story of Toussaint L'Ouverture. Born a slave, Toussaint educated himself in the library of a plantation owner, for whom he drove a carriage, and eventually became the leader in Haiti's struggle for freedom. He is the main figure in Obin's *Toussaint L'Ouverture Receiving a Message from the First Governor* (page 218). The French envoy in a gray suit, with his three-cornered hat under his arm, holds up a reddish-brown scroll. Toussaint, in a splendid uniform, is pictured as a black Napoleon with the same dictatorial airs. The black lady at his side, with a shy, friendly child, is no doubt the hero's wife. In the background are palms and red birds. This harmonious composition is painted flatly in transparent gray, blue, wine-red, and velvety green.

Wilson Bigaud is another painter in the group around Hyppolite. He paints Biblical compositions and scenes of popular life. His *Murder in the Jungle* of 1950 (page 217) shows a tropical forest very unlike those created by Henri Rousseau. It depicts an attack of savages armed with clubs on a group of men and women who have been picking fruit. Brilliantly colored parrots and birds of paradise are witnesses to this scene of murder and rape. Wilson Bigaud has also painted a *Marriage at Cana* in the Episcopal church of Port-au-Prince.

This mural is part of a large community project carried out in 1950 by the art center of Haiti. A number of talented popular artists contributed to the decoration of the church. The shoemaker and taxicab driver Rigaud Benoit (page 216) painted a *Nativity*, and the young Prefete Dufaut, a *Temptation of Christ*.

Gesnerr Abelard, a mechanic, began to paint still lifes and scenes of popular life at the industrial school of Port-au-Prince. His *Dining Room* (page 219) reveals a subtle sense for ornamental stylization and an ability to transmute real things into decorative colors. There are plants, flowers, ears of corn, asparagus, radishes; no spot is left unfilled, no space left for air. Colors and forms have combined to make a rich two-dimensional tapestery of charming naïveté.

This art of Haiti, intermediate between folklore and Sunday painting, has only very recently made its appearance. As late as 1938, M. J. Herkovits wrote in his book *Life in a Haitian Valley* that, except for wall decorations, crosses on graves, and carnival masks, the island possessed hardly anything resembling art.

Newly awakened popular artistic talents are also found in Latin American countries. Antonio J. Velasquez, telegraph worker and barber, depicts the life and history of San Antonio de Oriente, his town in the hills of Honduras, with meticulous pre-cision and delicate brushwork (pages 220, 221). The monastery church, with its white towers in the Spanish Baroque style, stands at the center of his world. It is in a dark green wood, and cobbled streets lead up to it. We see scattered figures—a donkey led by by a farm laborer, women, a child, and the village priest. In his somewhat rigid, simplified pictures, Velasquez depicts the eternal and unique face of San Antonio de Oriente with feeling, instinct, and application.

Asilia Guillén, who is an embroiderer by trade, lives in Managua, Nicaragua. Her native town, Granada, was once set afire by American marines, and she painted this memorable event (colorplate, page 103). Down a broad road, khaki-clad marines move through the woods, carrying their guns and torches. Houses and churches are already burning. At the bottom, near the river, there is a tablet with the inscription: "Here stood Granada!" People fleeing from their houses—men, women, and children—run down to the river. Successive phases of the event are juxtaposed. The distant figures on the hill are of the same size as those nearest to the viewer on the riverbank. The color is applied in tiny strokes that bring to mind the threads in an embroidery pat-

tern. The atmosphere of terror is conveyed by the motif rather than by the treatment. The figures are like little dolls, and the orange-colored blaze which illumines the scene of flight and despair is as though embroidered on silk. The picture reflects a childlike sensibility, but it is vigorously expressive.

Mario Urteaga is a native of Cajamarca in Peru. He exhibited for the first time in 1934, and three years later was awarded first prize at an international competition in Viño del Mar, Chile. The Museum of Modern Art in New York acquired the painting *Burial of an Illustrious Man* (colorplate, page 105), which he executed in 1936. The event is treated in a simple style, with subdued colors, and is tragic in feeling. Against a background of gray-blue, light-pink, and ivory-yellow houses, the funeral procession is passing by. At the center is the brown coffin resting on a litter, carried by men who are probably the village notables, and preceded by drummers and trumpeters. Hand-knit or woven garments supply spots of red in the picture; otherwise, everything is brown—the coffin, the baldachin, the clothes, the hats, and the shoes. Gravediggers on horseback hold their shovels over their shoulders like guns. The men's faces are solemn, and their

features express grief—we cannot tell whether real or ceremonial. The musicians in their soft hats may belong to another class of people or, even, race.

Urteagas' drawing is hard and clear. The ponderous primitivism of his forms is characteristic of his art; his noble colors recall the finely woven costumes of Inca mummies.

Felicindo Iglesias y Acevedo, a grocer and wine merchant in Cuba, was born in Spain. In his spare time he sings and plays the organ in a church in Havana. In 1939 he began to paint enamel-like compositions, which, in their simple piety, remind us of medieval altarpieces. One of his works, *The Discovery of Cuba by Christopher Columbus*, possesses a visionary quality, for all its awkwardness. The composition moves us, despite the poor technique, by its intensity: we feel the sublimity of Columbus' perilous adventure.

One more important naïve artist of the American continent may be mentioned—the Mexican José Guadalupe Posada. Born at Aguascalientes in 1851, he belonged to an older generation than ours; he was more or less a contemporary of Joseph Pickett. This primitive master drew upon themes buried

deep in the popular mind, appealing to the broad masses of the people in the graphic medium. He contributed greatly to the awakening of modern art in Mexico. In 1878, Posada, tired of his life as a schoolteacher, moved from Léon to Mexico City. Here he began to produce those prints of *corridos*, *ejemplos*, and *calaveras*, which, with their spontaneity and vitality, have remained a vivid, frequently humorous chronicle of the life of the Mexican nation. He produced about fifteen thousand prints in all, etched on zinc plates or engraved in iron or type metal. Touching or sensational events are made understandable to an illiterate population in the black-and-white language of prints such as the one shown below. Gambling with death, brutality, romanticism, aggressive realisme, folk humor, sadness—all these elements of the Mexican soul are reflected in his work. The funeral ornaments of pre-Columbian sculpture and the dance-of-death allegories of the Spanish Colonial Baroque are here combined with dramatic narrative talent. Posada could hold his audience with the skill of a village storyteller.

When Posada died in 1913, his work was still completely unknown to the world at large. Twenty

José Guadalupe Posada:
Liberal Politician Addressing Crowd

years later the Mexican painter Charlot discovered Posada's plates, and produced prints from them that he published and exhibited. Long before the monumental frescoes of the Mexican national style were painted, Posada had given expression to the Spanish-Indian epic in realistic, popular prints of lapidary grandeur. Thereby, he exerted a strong influence on the future art of his country, as the Douanier Rousseau did in France.

The totemic emblems of the dawn of mankind and the modern ghosts of technology are today closely juxtaposed on the continents and islands of America. The voodoo demons in the paintings of the Haitian artist Gourgue appear in the cool light of television; the tiger with black and yellow stripes from the psychoanalytic Mother Goose book of Morris Hirshfield pads soundlessly under Calder's metal trees, swaying in the draft of the air conditioner. Alongside the calculations of electronic brains, we find the metaphysical speculations of untutored philosophers like Patrick J. Sullivan and Theora Hamblett. In the day of mass-produced color photographs, Grandma Moses paints her cheerful, motherly landscapes in the colors of the soul. Parallel to an abstract art of still-uninventoried forms and still-unnamed things is discernible a still-surviving primordial magic, the art of a "greater reality," as Kandinsky termed it, in the paintings of the American primitives of today.

Mankind slowly but steadily takes back the psychic projections that had filled the world's emptiness with hierarchies of gods and spirits, heavens and hells, and is amazed to discover the creative richness of its own primeval psychic ground.

Erich Neumann, Tiefenpsychologie

VIII The Peasant Painters of Yugoslavia

The naïve artists of Yugoslavia still draw (even though in most cases unconsciously) upon the subterranean currents of folk art. The past has not been wiped out completely: the Bogomile sarcophagi, Serbian peasant tombstones, carved shepherds' stocks, knitted or woven peasant cloths, and votive paintings on glass have survived down to our day. A residue of communal feelings and collective life still finds expression in naïve art, although in Yugoslavia, too, the advance of industrialization is driving out traditional forms and ways of seeing and has almost killed them off. The last remnants of patriarchal tradition may well be responsible for one very special phenomenon: the schools of painting in the villages of Hlebine and Kovačica.

Ivan Generalić is the central figure of the school at Hlebine, which was founded when Generalić, as a sixteen-year-old peasant boy, met the Zagreb artist Krsto Hegedušić. Previously, in 1929, Hegedušić with a number of other Croatian artists had founded the group Zemlia ("Earth"). This group believed that modern art was declining, that its irrationality and obscurity cut it off from the people, and that only the people could instill new life into it. In the village of Hlebine, Hegedušić discovered talented artists who still drew strength from their native soil. The peasants Generalić and Mraz formed the nucleus of a group of painters; these were joined first by Mirko Virius, and later by a number of younger artists—Dolenc, Gaži, Filipović, and Večenaj. Thus there came into being a peasant community that believed that man's nourishment must include, besides the fruits of the earth, the fruits of the creative imagination as exemplified in works of art. Eventually Hlebine—the village of painters—became a place of pilgrimage for all art lovers.

The meeting between the artist Hegedušić and the peasant Generalić turned out to be more significant than the two painters themselves realized. As a result of this meeting Hegedušić, a trained artist, became friend and helper to the naïve peasant painter, who heretofore had relied on feeling alone. By this means, Hegedušić himself crossed the barrier separating art from the people. As a teacher, the trained artist learned a great deal, and was stimulated by the unspoiled instinct of his peasant pupils.

To understand an artist, it is usually sufficient to study his works. With the peasant painters, however, life and work are inseparable. These naïve artists are not concerned with pure aesthetics. In their paintings, they record their daily labors and occasional celebrations—christenings, weddings, funerals—their devotion to the earth, and their rebellion against the excessive burdens imposed on them. Their works are vigorous, reflecting their native shrewdness and naïve poetic vision.

Even as a boy, when he tended pigs, Ivan Generalić kept pencil and paper in his pocket, to be able to sketch, whenever he had a free moment, the things that he saw, felt, or imagined. His early works are like children's drawings with their unexpected rhythms and sharpness. Their clear outlines transcend the boundaries of logic; the real and the imaginary are treated as equivalents. Shepherds, dogs, snow, dark woods, trees, and animals are all represented with equal candor and poetic precision. He conveys graphically the despair of the peasant whose cow is confiscated by a tax collector.

The *Burial of Štef Halachek* (colorplate, page 113), we are told, is merely a crude practical joke. Štef Halachek was still alive when the artist put him in a coffin and surrounded his body with grieving relatives. There they stand in the snowy country-side—friends, acquaintances, and the priest—stiff and cold, as though carved of wood. Dream and reality, laughter and tragedy, paralyzing grief and grotesque peasant vitality are combined to create a kind of legend.

Generalić's still lifes have a monumental quality. One shows nothing but a loaf of bread and an earthenware pitcher, another a plucked chicken lying wretchedly naked, pale, and very dead. Through a small window we see the vast expanse of the fertile fields of Croatia. Other works depict country dances (page 224) and farm laborers plowing the fields. One of his favorite subjects is village fires. The night lies over the village like a dark-blue velvet blanket. The salmon-red eyes of the fire flick at the windows of the burning house. Pails of water are passed from hand to hand, and men on ladders are screaming. A Brueghel-like tale is told with robust energy and poetic concentration. A deer in coral-pink woods and a scene of horses fighting in a broad plain are similarly transported to dream regions real beyond reality itself.

Ivan Generalić has done many paintings on glass (see page 222). He has mastered this technique, which, even when practiced with the greatest virtuosity, always contains elements of the unforeseen and accidental. The colors are vibrant with feeling—the dark-green shimmer of the meadows, the dull-yellow veins in the ghostly trees, the gently modulated white of the shepherds' cloaks, the golden brown and brick reds of autumn foliage. But for all the candor of the statement, his sense of space and proportion stand out. Visitors to Hlebine today will still find Ivan Generalić and his people there. "I still live in the village," he says, "and I paint when I have time, when there is no work in the fields—that is to say, in the winter, on rainy days, and on Sundays."

The lyrical pastel-like landscapes of Franjo Mraz lack Generalić's vigor and precise drawing. This artist's earlier paintings on glass disclose him as a sensitive observer of life. With awkward hands, Mraz created an austerely poetic world, but he was dissatisfied with his work. He set out upon the endless, dangerous, yet tempting journey to a more sophisticated art. He left his village and nibbled at the tree of academic knowledge. He learned a great deal, but in the process lost much of his spontaneity.

Next to Generalić, the most gifted painter of the school was, beyond doubt, Mirko Virius. He often preferred to paint on canvas rather than on glass. He loved pigment and he had a feeling for the fullness of life, which he wanted to record with truth and vigor. Because he identified with the things that he painted, and he shared their life, his art is dramatic and realistic. He painted himself in a vineyard: he has the hands of a workingman, with short broad fingernails, and serious questioning eyes, which try to take in everything that life holds— everything that he has seen and experienced in the fields and in the village.

His peasants go calmly about their heavy tasks— plowing, mowing, binding the sheaves, hoeing—in sunshine or rain. Their faces, with long mustaches, are stiff, big-nosed, wrinkled; and their strong hands, like his own, are used to work. He often depicts homely dramas of the fields. For example, two peasants have a quarrel, turning their backs upon theirs horses, cows, and plows. One peasant strikes the other over the head with a stick, catching him off balance, and the latter lies stunned, looking helplessly up at the sky.

Virius gives us no bucolic idylls, no didactic illustrations of peasant proverbs. He depicts the existence of peasants with stark realism, from his own personal observation and experience (page 231). His vigorous, expressive outlines convey a somber mood of rebellion. His paintings may express a protest against social injustice and against his lost years as a prisoner of war; perhaps there is also foreboding that he will not live long. In the spring of 1936 his works were exhibited for the first time, along with those of Generalić and Mraz. "This encouraged me to pick up my pencil a little more often. Now I doodle with the pencil like any other child, big or little." Virius was murdered in 1943, in the concentration camp of Zemun.

Younger painters have also come out of Hlebine, the village touched by the spirit of art; and many have come from other villages to study under Generalić.

Franjo Filipović paints scenes from the everyday repertoire of peasant life in vigorous, cheerful,

Ivan Generalić: Burial of Štef Halachek

folksy colors: the baking of bread, a dinner table, a duck hunter in a boat (page 227), water plants in a swampy region. His drawing is simplified and spontaneous; the colors, applied in large areas, look as though cut out of shiny paper and pasted on the canvas.

Dragan Gaži constructs colorful flat landscapes and portrays old men and women in paintings on glass. His faces are unforgettable—for instance, that of a woman in candlelight, with tremulous outlines the color of earth, and wrinkles like furrows in a field, or the face in *Dijak's Aunt*, dark, suffering, the closed eyes suggesting devotion and prayer. Gaži's fully resonant colors remind us of old German masters. But there can be no doubt that he is an authentic peasant painter. One of his works depicts a party—a low-ceilinged room at an inn, with dancing couples, drinkers with pitchers and wine, a bride in a white veil. Everything is sharply outlined, rigid, and solemn.

The young peasant Mijo Kovačić says: "I heard that the peasant Ivan Generalić of the village of Hlebine was practicing the art of painting. So I went to him and showed him my drawings and water-colors. He looked at them and began to give me lessons."

Kovačić paints the green village landscape as a life of agreeable labor—with scarcely a trace of effort. In one picture (page 225) we see a villager under a tree, ocher-colored sheaves of wheat, and a cow grazing on the part of the field that has already been harvested, alongside the ripe grain stalks in full splendor—a moment of plenitude and prosperity.

Ivan Večenaj has painted Madonna-faced women feeding geese in the farmyard, and also the afternoon stillness of thatched peasant dwellings. Another painting (page 229) shows a man, mowing by hand, who has laid down his scythe to take a refreshing draught from an earthenware pitcher. The land around him stretches in strips of cultivation like the pleats in a skirt.

Večenaj has set a cattle market in a landscape of bluish snow, with a dark-gray sky and cadmium-yellow houses. The colorful aprons, shawls, and horse blankets endow the scene with the cheerful animation of peasant rugs. The human figures, the horse, the cow, and the calf all wear the same expression—that of innocent children.

The peasant Martin Mehkek of the village of Novačka near Gola depicts men carrying troughs— forsaken figures woodenly rigid in their expressions. They bring to mind the charcoal burners portrayed by Grimmelshausen in the seventeenth century.

The peasant Slavko Stolnik now wears the uniform of the People's Militia. Nevertheless he has a very nonmilitary fondness for painting. The fertility of his invention is surprising. His memory overflows with anecdotes, both gay and tragic, which he always depicts vividly and amusingly. Quickly sketched and colored in sparkling bright tones, his paintings on glass disclose a tendency to the caricatural and illustrative.

Mato Skurjeni, a house painter, is also of peasant extraction. He does not see the world as a gay, colorful place, but as a landscape permeated with the pungent smells of earth and sweat. His paintings are of a harsh, monotonous simplicity. Nor are his skies evocative of paradise; rather, they are darkened by the smoke of railway trains, drawn as though by a child, making their way across bleak landscapes like those around modern cities.

As Eugen Buktenica's native island of Šolta in the Adriatic Sea appears in his works—houses, church, cypresses, fields, and behind them the expanses of sea and sky—it is a sight to lift the heart and broaden our horizons. He is clearly unlike the naïve painters of the mainland. Peasant and fisherman, Buktenica has an innate sense of form, which may have something to do with his native landscape. His fishing boats, with the gray limestone mountains in the distance over the blue sea, bring to mind the votive paintings of sailors (see page 227). Perhaps even more naïve is the cheerful view of the port Tatinja, with a couple in a boat and a group of workers at a lime kiln against a background of sea and steamboats, which relieve the severity of the brick kiln.

Buktenica has also painted a holiday procession with the carnival king on horseback holding a scepter in the shape of a bull's head, a man in a boat holding Neptune's trident, and a herald blowing his trumpet (colorplate, page 223). These figures might be portraying a legend from some long dead age; the meaning of the symbols has been forgotten, but they are still preserved in the carnival celebrations of the fishermen. In another of Buktenica's paintings, a shepherdess is tending black and white sheep on a green meadow embroidered with flowers under a fruit tree in blossom, in a setting of limestone cliffs. In the background is an olive grove, and the cloudless Mediterranean sky. We are reminded of the frescoes in Slavic monasteries of the East, where the saints are depicted standing on the green earth, for they are of earthly origin, but reaching into the blue sky to which they have ascended.

Buktenica combines large simplified outlines with restrained, light colors, transmuting reality and idealizing it into legend. In his nonperspective two-dimensional pictures, things and human figures become symbols of inner experiences.

Hlebine in Croatia is not the only village of painters in Yugoslavia. A second school of painters has grown up at Kovačica, a village in the Banat. Here workers and peasants exhibit together in a permanent gallery in the local House of Culture. Their modestly framed little pictures are hung on walls and screens; some of them are decorated with gold braid. The primitive art of the peasant painters of Kovačica is rooted in tradition. Their range of color brings to mind the syncopated rhythms characteristic of Slovak folk songs. This attachment to tradition may derive its strength from the fact that they are a distinct ethnic group. Their art has the friendliness and vitality of simple people who express their emotions and experiences without affectation.

Martin Paluška has painted Kovačica in the spring—white geese on meadows green as billiard cloth, and a plain Baroque church, such as are found in this region, standing stiff and prim as though cut out of cardboard. Paluška has also painted the house where he was born, set among soft trees swaying in the breeze, like those in Grimm's fairy tales. Only the telegraph poles remind us that we are not in fairyland. A portrait of his wife in her peasant blouse shows her wearing a kerchief decorated with asters. Her face peeps out as though through the curtain of a Russian vaudeville theater.

Jano Strakušek, peasant and mason, says that he uses colors as his building blocks. He has pictured himself, his companions, his village in winter, and the living room of his friend Jano Sokol, another peasant painter. Sokol's wife, in this last painting, is at the spinning wheel in front of a large tile stove. Two children are seen in profile under a calendar on the wall, which has been painted so meticulously that we can almost read the date. Everything visible—people, furniture, the flower patterns on the women's dresses and on the wallpaper—has been set down painstakingly and with frank joy in living.

Paluška and Sokol were the first painters in this community. Over the years, other painters have gathered around them—peasants, both old and young, who have found pleasure in being able to give expression to their thoughts and feelings in paint.

Jano Sokol has painted an interior scene of a bride getting ready for the wedding ceremony. Dressed in stiffly starched lace, and looking like some inanimate toy, she stands before an open closet while her attendants wait in the doorway. Their faces look as though cut from old cookie molds. The artist has also painted village scenes. One shows boys and girls sitting on wooden benches along the walls of a room; while the boys play accordions, the girls pluck fowl. Another shows a wedding procession, the girls walking ahead in their brilliant garb, the men following (page 231). These events seem to be taking place in some other day, long ago. And it is true that the peasants have clung to old ways to a far greater extent than have people in the cities.

The children's dance depicted by Jano Knjazović is perhaps even more evocative of the past (page 230). Against the background of a luminous blue wall, boys are whirling their girls around. The full skirts stand out flying. Two musicians with their instruments are in the background. On a bench by the stove a little boy and a little girl sit apart from the rest; their feet do not even reach to the red-brown floor. The cheerful colors of the folk costumes endow the scene with charm and directness. The dancers are caught as though frozen in time—like some moment of an underseas ballet in deep blue water.

The naïve painters of Kovačica often seem stiff because of the almost pedantic meticulousness with which they set down what they see. But this stiffness is part of their vision. The traditional folklore element is preserved in their works to a far greater extent than in those of the peasants of Hlebine. In the works of the latter, it is only the technique of painting on glass that is traditional.

The peasant painters of Serbia, unlike those of Croatia, do not know the technique of glass painting. No school of art like that of Hlebine or Kovačica has developed in the Serbian village of Šumadija. The peasants are artistically inclined, but they work on their own; by temperament they are individualists. Perhaps the most fertile creative talent among them is that of Janko Brašić of the village of Oparić.

To get to where he lives involves a long ride over rough country. He has an authentic old farm with several buildings, one of which serves as a workshop where the painter makes his own frames. The garden is full of flowers. And Čika Janko, as the painter is familiarly called, is a slender, wiry man with a thin face and pale, gentle eyes. According to the old Serbian custom, the entire "greater family" lives together on the farm, but the younger generation will go on to college and set up its own establishments.

The painter wears the national costume of homespun brown woolen cloth. He began to draw as a schoolboy; later he learned to make his own paints from plant juices. One whole wall of his studio is occupied by his *Battle Between the Serbs and Turks* (page 228). This is a large composition depicting, in extremely realistic detail, lurid scenes of violence: men choking each other with their bare hands and attacking each other with swords, knives, and farm tools. There is a conscious effort to achieve a monumental art. The tumultuous scene, disarming in its literalness, is a forceful portrayal of man's cruelty to man, and reflects the artist's Serbian patriotism. Janko Brašić is the only naïve painter in Yugoslavia who prefers large-scale compositions. In this, he may have been influenced by medieval frescoes, many of which have survived in the churches and monasteries of his region. Incidentally, he decorated his village church with murals.

Nonetheless, he remains a self-taught artist and a sharp-eyed observer of the rough and robust life around him. He has painted men brawling in a tavern, soldiers on guard duty shivering with cold on a winter night, a scene of burial, and a folk dance called the Kolo (page 230). Almost all the dancers have identical solemn faces, only the mustaches distinguishing the men's from the women's. The colors are harsh and shrill, the poses frozen, as in posters for a country fair.

The paintings by his pupil, the peasant Miroslav Marinković, are like embroidered wall hangings. The modulated decorative colors are held within naïve vigorous outlines, Houses, meadows, woods, clouds, human faces, and flocks of sheep are treated with equal emphasis and are interwoven, as in a tapestry.

A similar childlike expressiveness characterizes *Village Wedding* by the peasant Cvetan Belić (page 232), executed with painstaking technique. The festive table and the figures in front of it are firmly outlined and shrilly colored. We see the mother wiping her eyes, the bride and groom and the witnesses, a bagpipe player, and a girl holding candles. On the wall an image of the patron saint is framed in embroidered cloth, and through the window next to it, we see the splendid horses that draw the bridal carriage. The painting is remarkable for its deformations and for the figures shown in frontal view or profile, frozen in ceremonial attitudes.

In Macedonia, near Lake Ohrid, the honorable tradition of woodcarving is cultivated in peasant workshops. Vangel Naumovski, who has worked as gardener, mason, coachmaker, and lemonade vendor, and who is now a designer of pseudo-Baroque furniture, spends his spare time composing pictures inspired by popular songs, legends, and riddles. *Death of Kuzman Ohried* (page 226), painted in romantic colors, shows a group of women mourning,

a white-haired old man at the door of the dead hero's house, the three men who have brought back the body, and a white horse. Though unmistakably modern in conception, the work has archaic overtones. Several of Naumovski's paintings convey the epic quality of the collective soul, but his technique is sure, almost virtuoso at times; artistic consciousness has already impaired native innocence.

So far, the peasant painters we have discussed are primarily inspired by nature. Not so Emerik Feješ. He is a button-and-comb manufacturer. Like all city dwellers he dreams of faraway places. With the help of picture post cards his imagination journeys to fantastic realms, the architecture of which is a mosaic of his own dreams. There was less emphasis upon fantastic structures in his early works. *The Garden* (colorplate, page 121) reminds us a bit of the village scenes in Chagall's pictures, which Feješ never saw. This picture shows a family among its possessions. But where Chagall is the eternal wanderer, storyteller, and inventor, Feješ meticulously enumerates detail. There is little sky here, and a great deal of earth. We see the inside of the house, the front wall having been removed. A man is fanning the fire under a pot suspended by a chain from the ceiling. He is surrounded by a table, bed, stool, pail, and watering can, none of these shown in perspective. Outside, there are haystacks, and the meadow is of a summer yellow, like the golden ground of an icon. At the bottom we see children in the grass, lambs, geese, a horse and carriage, a woman at her washtub, and a dog. The people and the animals are very much like each other—another variety of archaism. The houses have a life of their own, their colors and forms bursting with innocent vitality.

Emerik Feješ' city views are those of a world traveler who has hardly ever left his room—veritable orgies of the imagination. The little dabs of color with which he composes his mosaic world disclose his innermost thoughts. The narrow Gothic gables of Amsterdam, which soar lacily above the canals, are painted in wine-red, emerald, and sea-blue colors. The sepia and red towers of the Palazzo Vecchio loom against a dark sky, and St. Mark's in Venice shimmers like a precious enamel box. Tiny horse-drawn cabs are lined up as in times long past in front of the provincial Baroque houses of Novi Sad, the city where he lives. A view of Subotica (page 233), another city of the Voivodina, shows the imposing façade of a house with sculptural orna-ments, including the city's coat of arms, and windows of different colors. The telegraph wires to the right and left, high above the street, are carrying messages from faraway places.

Feješ' world is built up brick by brick. His views of it are based on secondhand prints, old illustrated magazines, and picture post cards. In the little room that serves as his studio, he keeps them all around him. He looks at his visitor through dark-rimmed glasses and speaks nervously: "I have painted most of my pictures with matches," he says. Indeed, matches dipped in the shrill colors of his dreams have until recently served him as paint brushes; with them he painted his zebra-striped churches, his endless rows of houses, and his palaces of the ideal.

Jean Cassou, when I showed him Feješ' pictures, agreed with me that they bear an amazing affinity to those of Louis Vivin. Like Vivin, the post-office clerk, Feješ paints every detail lovingly. To him, houses, palaces, streets, and cities are the carefully kept file cabinet of human existence.

The fact that peasants, fishermen, and artisans in many regions of Yugoslavia are not content just to till their fields, cast their nets, and work with their

Emerik Feješ: The Garden

everyday tools, surely points to the existence of an inner need. They try to give imaginative expression to their vision of life, as if they knew that spiritual nourishment is as indispensable as daily bread.

Because they are strongly rooted in their native soil, their works similarly go deep and reveal that primitive and traditional elements still shape their lives. At the same time, they have begun to feel the effects of modern civilization.

What these peasant artists signify, perhaps, is a stage in history between the archaic patriarchal society and the scientifically planned society, the contrast between a dying world and a world being born. Their creative search is both disturbed and stimulated by the circumstance that, historically and sociologically, they find themselves between moribund communal traditions and intimations of new forms of collective life.

IX Naïve Lyricism
Elsewhere in Europe

It is scarcely surprising that public interest was aroused in simple, nonintellectual representations of reality at a moment when professional artists had turned their backs on natural visual appearance and had embarked on formal analysis. The primitive painters of the twentieth century have restored our vision of things as we see them, and have made it possible once again to take lyrical delight in what is about us. They are concerned solely with recording reality, and are unaffected by the changing styles and successive schools of modern art. Much as children in their drawings transform the world around them into a garden of magical properties, so modern primitive artists transform the reality that they seek to record, both by the innocence of their vision and the crudeness of their technique. Forms

123

and the relations among forms are simplified; details are lingered over almost to the point of abstraction. In the process, the ordinary appearances of things take on the quality of legend or fable.

It has not been only in France that the painting of nonprofessional artists, of the past as well as of the present, has been "discovered" and its importance recognized. In Germany, the works of several early primitive painters were rescued from oblivion by N. Michailov. Among these artists are J. Kiessinger of Hallstatt, a salt worker; Johann Jakob Hauswirth, a charcoal burner; and Eduard Gisevius, who taught school at Tilsit. Michailov was especially enthusiastic about the works of Oluf Braren, who was born in 1787 on the island of Föhr in the North Sea, and taught school for a living. His paintings are described as the most important achievement among all the earlier nonprofessional artists. Franz Roh, the art historian, has said of Braren: "In my opinion, this remarkable tragic figure marks the high point of German nonprofessional painting before the twentieth century."

Son of a blacksmith, Oluf Braren became a teacher against his father's wishes. Unhappy in his marriage, he defied convention and lived with his mistress, by whom he had children. In 1822 he lost his position as teacher and led the life of an outcast, depending for support on his brother and on occasional commissions. He died of tuberculosis at the age of fifty-two. It is possible that his poverty and unhappiness enhanced his native gifts for expression and drove him to pour out his heart in his paintings.

He collected plants, stones, and shells, studied the beauty and order inherent in these things, and made drawings of them. In addition, he painted portraits that were vigorous in color, and graceful even though stiff, as well as a few figurative compositions. In the latter, it would seem that he carried over to his depiction of human figures what he had learned about mussels, plants, and geological formations. His portraits and groups (particularly two paintings representing private weddings) have crystalline clarity: the faces are painted as though they were flowers or stones. This rigid monumentality can be accounted for only partly by contemporaneous classicism. It is rather more akin to Hans Baldung Grien and Lucas Cranach.

Private Wedding, Föhr (page 236) depicts a solemn ceremony. The bride and the groom are at the right, with the pastor. The guests, in old-fashioned costumes meticulously rendered, look on attentively.

Each of the sharply outlined figures is self-contained —an effect strengthened by the metallic glow of the colors. This terse austerity in defining natural appearance is both realistic and magical, naïve and inspired.

Except for Braren, German nonprofessional painting has not produced talents of the first rank. On the whole, it shows tendencies toward whimsicality, eccentricity, humor, and sentimentality, rather than toward striking presentation of reality or poetic symbolism.

Braren's accurate rendering of regional costumes in color introduced an ethnic note into German painting. Jan Arndt Boëtius, a baker who lived in Wyk, also on the island of Föhr, faithfully depicted the people and costumes of the North Sea islands, in a style characterized by limpid, severe colored planes. Christian Peter Hansen, who was born and grew up on Sylt, an island of the North Sea, was Braren's friend and pupil. He was an earnest student of local history and an enthusiastic collector; he painted both landscapes and portraits. His portrait of a girl on her wedding day has a quality of poetic candor that suggests that he was not unacquainted with works of the German Romantic painters, such as Kaspar David Friedrich. These un-

trained artists of the North Sea islands lived in surroundings where houses and customs of the past had often been preserved, and they realized the value and significance of them. During the long winter months, when they were cut off from the outside world, they could develop and improve their art at leisure.

Among the next generation of German naïve artists, perhaps the most original was Adalbert Trillhaase (page 240), born at Erfurt in 1859. He was by temperament a dreamer who, despite youthful apprenticeship to a merchant, was unsuccessful in practical affairs. Such business ventures as a linen factory and a metal workshop ended in failure. He began to paint at the age of fifty-nine, choosing historical or Biblical scenes as his favorite subjects. His compositions are reminiscent of Bauchant (whose works he never saw), and his fantastic style has nothing in common with the folk tradition followed by village artist-schoolmasters. His paintings are unconscious attempts to express and interpret his dreams in color and line. Although the subjects chosen are familiar, his art invests them with a ghostly character that has nothing to do with the events narrated. In a painting showing Abraham about to sacrifice his son Isaac, the patriarch's broad-featured, bearded, earnest face has a prophetic sublimity. The unconscious protest of his heart and the instinctive hesitation of his conscience are embodied in the angel who orders him to halt the sacrifice. In another of his paintings we see Cain standing rigid, with upraised hands and twisted face, after murdering his brother. Here we feel that this is indeed the first criminal, who set in motion an endless cycle of destruction and revenge. A third painting shows the Witch of Endor summoning up the spirit of Samuel, which prophesies doom to King Saul.

In these works, the figures of Abraham, Cain, and the ancient seeress are set apart from the other figures in the composition. They are carrying on their own private dialogue with God, with their consciences, or with fate. These allegorical paintings are technically imperfect, but they are striking for their curious mixture of faith and superstition, as illustrations of a demonology. The artist seems to have created them in a state of trance, in obedience to voices that he alone could hear.

Carl Christian Thegen (page 239) is a very different artist. His drawings and paintings are as unstudied as a child's. Without critical inhibitions or control,

he recorded everything he had ever seen or experienced: a merry-go-round, a gypsy family, the graceful movements of a circus rider, the melancholy cheerfulness of a clown, the appearance of an exotic herd. He very often painted animals, and as with his human figures, these are given strictly in profile.

Thegen, a native of the Lübeck region, learned the butcher's trade. At the age of nineteen he became a clown in a traveling circus, and, later, was employed by the Hagenbeck circus as an animal attendant. Still later he owned and operated a merry-go-round. His successive occupations are all documented in his pictures.

His paintings are expressive in their cheerful, lighthearted way. He was particularly skillful in his depiction of animals; living with them as he did, he was familiar with every stage of their lives, from birth on. In broad, sweeping outlines, he drew such animals as horses, buffaloes, sheep, giraffes, and tigers in a great variety of poses—grazing, chewing their cud, and attacking other animals.

Karl Kazmierczak (page 245), who began to paint at the age of sixty-four, has worked in the Thyssen steel mills. He is endowed with a sensibility that enables him, despite the scantiness of his technical means, to explore the nature of phenomena with considerable interest.

In his sixties, the locksmith Heinrich Schilling, who works in the Krupp factories in Essen, has produced landscapes of spontaneous expressive quality with primitively simplified color elements (page 245).

Johann Mis, who works for a mining company, paints scenes descriptive of his work, in a lively and simplified way.

These are only a few among many individual workers and miners who are today attempting to give their jobs meaning in terms of art. The German Federation of Labor encourages talented workers and artisans by organizing its own exhibitions. Thus, the people themselves serve as patrons of art. Similar aspirations guide the Austrian Federation of Labor in periodic exhibitions given under the title *Talente entdeckt-erweckt* (Talents Discovered-awakened)."

The cabinetmaker Hans Strygel of Baden, near Vienna, and the file cutter Franz A. Spielbichler of Lilienfeld, in Lower Austria, both paint vivid,

naïvely deformed portraits, as well as scenes of life in their native towns.

Not all the naïve painters come from the common people. The educated also take up art without previous study. Felix Muche, called Ramholz (page 242), seems to be one of these. He has paintings by Chagall, Picasso, Feininger, Franz Marc, and Paul Klee in his studio. He seems to have followed the complicated developments of modern art through many discussions of painting with his son, who taught at the Bauhaus. Impelled by his inner need, and inspired by a lively, amusing imagination, his works are as deliberately simple as they are attractive.

Similarly, it is only with respect to technique that Paps (colorplate, page 129; page 244) is grouped among the primitives. An educated man, he began to paint at the age of sixty-nine, after a long and busy career as a professional man. He creates an animated, naïve, harmonious world of richly nuanced colors. His landscapes and street scenes of faraway places that he visited in his youth, when he was a ship's surgeon, recall melodies from operas, which he likes to hum while painting. And Professor

Theodor Brugsch, the eighty-year-old director of the Humboldt University clinics in Berlin, and an outstanding diagnostician, is a naïve painter who expresses his love of the world and of things in poetic drawings and paintings.

There is even more deliberate simplicity in the paintings of the poet Joachim Ringelnatz, which describe scenes from his life both tragic and humorous. He traveled all over the world in his youth, first as a cabin boy and then as a sailor; he has also sold newspapers, decorated shop windows, worked as a salesman for a manufacturer of tar paper, and been a tourist guide. During the First World War he was an officer in the German navy. All these experiences are reflected in his poems and "Sunday" paintings. In *Experience* (1925) a man is shown running away while a girl stands weeping under a tree; the feelings of solitude, guilt, and fear are well rendered. *Snake Charmer or the Victim* is an exotic scene with palm trees and the dazzlingly white sail of a boat (page 241).

The tiny dark figures in *Festival Season* sway in the same rhythm as the dark silhouettes of the houses, as if the whole scene were being shaken by an earthquake. His *Heavenly Bridge* is like a rainbow over a fantastic mist-covered landscape. Pedestrians and carriages alike seem to be moving toward some destination that they will never reach. His *Childhood* has terrifying implications: a tiny creature is squatting between high stacks of lumber and a gray wall, as though imprisoned in a tomb. *Bored* shows a couple who have nothing to say to each other, in a landscape that is as alien to them as they are to each other.

Ringelnatz, the songster who used to comment on the imperfection of the world with a glass of wine in his hand, was also an artist whose ballad-like paintings were prophetic of the rising forces of evil in Germany. *Flight*, executed in 1933, shows a prisoner with his face pressed against the bars, dreaming of escape and freedom. In his imagination he is sailing off in a winged boat; a songbird in a cage and a goldfish in its aquarium symbolize his dream of escape. Another painting of the same year, *On the Brink*, expresses tragic foreboding: a baby carriage is shown at the very edge of a steep cliff, at the foot of which angry waves are beating. For all their intellectual content and conscious Surrealism, these symbolic paintings are the spontaneous works of a sensitive amateur.

With such artists, we find it hard to be sure whether we are dealing with genuine naïveté or with a more deliberate simplicity. Georgy Stefula (page 243), who often exhibits with naïve painters, but whose attractive pictures reveal him as a skillful artist, represents another kind of art: that of the professional painter who deliberately employs the naïve forms of the authentic primitives.

Stefula paints pink and lemon-yellow houses adorned with tiny towers, toylike monuments to heroes, and slumbering city squares. Little pansies are lined up in a row, as though they were looking out a window. His works are quite consciously composed with respect to both their fantastic and ironical elements. Stefula's tight-rope walkers, performing alone in a wood at night, with trees shimmering in the moonlight around them, prove once again that he is a skillful artist, familiar with Surrealism, who has chosen to work in the spontaneous idiom of the naïve.

In Switzerland, a naïve painting rooted firmly in folklore traditions was practiced as early as the eighteenth century. At first, it consisted merely of the decoration of objects of daily use—chests and cupboards, for instance. Later, landscapes and portraits of farmers and shepherds appeared, and, occasionally, an individual artist's name became known. Bartholomäus Laemmler was the best known of these early folk painters. His numerous scenes of shepherd life disclose a feeling for rhythm, color, and form. His herds of black cows and flocks of white sheep are aligned like the figures of Egyptian friezes, and the alternately light and dark shapes that they form provide a kind of embroidery on the green Alpine pastures.

In the nineteenth century, this vigorous popular art gave way to the souvenir industry for tourists—a pseudo-folk art. Not until the turn of the century did interest in primitives reawaken. Among contemporary naïve painters in Switzerland, the most important is Adolf Dietrich (colorplate, page 133). Son of a small farmer, he has worked as a farmhand and a factory worker. Although accustomed to heavy manual labor, he has preserved a sensibility that enables him to depict his small world with microscopic accuracy and childlike delight in creation. His gardens and fruits, stuffed birds, martens, mice, and people are defined with the plastic intensity of a *quattrocento* artist and the directness of a primitive. His still lifes of flowers, animal paintings, self-portraits, and portraits of other persons are characterized by drawing as meticulous as that of the old masters, and his color reflects the delicately subdued palette of the German Romantics. He is genuinely a naïve painter, unfamiliar with the academic canon. His technical skill was acquired by years of hard work. He conveys wonder at the magical stillness of things, by his predilection for the minute detail. He is a pantheistic poet and interpreter of life, aware of the harmony and beauty of ordinary little things to be found everywhere in nature.

Miguel G. Vivancos, a native of Murcia in Spain, was a chauffeur, a dock worker, a bricklayer, and a miner. He fought in the Spanish Civil War. For five years he was interned in a French refugee camp. After this experience he began to paint. He had been given a job involving painting on silk, but the stereotyped patterns bored him, and he tried to invent some of his own. Perhaps we should have listed him among the French naïve painters, on the principle that groups Juan Gris and Picasso with the School of Paris. His art was not only born in France; it is also French in inspiration. His *Country Fair* reproduces the gay and colorful forms of a French village that he has obviously known; we see the ordinary people wandering among the shooting galleries and merry-go-rounds, and there is a photographer with an enormous camera who puts his customers in front of a painted automobile so that they may pose as world travelers.

His *Still Life with Pheasant* (page 246) also reveals his predilection for the lyrical clash of luminous colors. The theatrically draped ultramarine silk curtain opens a rhetorical vista on a fairyland scene complete with a romantic castle. On the lace tablecloth, woven meticulously of white paint and patience, is the main figure—the golden pheasant in all its variegated plumage, painted with utter realism. The exuberant colors of the bird express joy in living—in marked contrast with the dead fowl by Ivan Generalić, already described, which is a definition of mortality. Vivanco's somewhat excessive love of magnificent colors is perhaps, after all, an expression of his Spanish heritage.

The very air of Italy is saturated with the patina of her glorious past. Any notion of the "primitive" in our sense is alien to Italy. There the cultural heritage reigns supreme; the pathos of antiquity and the harmony of the classical age can at most be "primitivized" only by being made provincial.

This cultural heritage is present even in the laborious brush strokes of the self-taught artists of Italy, even in the ponderous and awkward realism of her Sunday painters.

Among the artisans of Italy, particularly in the small towns, there have always been self-taught yet passionate artists who composed idealized pictures of the life about them—portraits, landscapes, genre scenes, and mythological glorifications of the land's many struggles for liberation over the centuries. Local museums and storerooms contain painted signs for taverns and painted booths for local fairs. These are of poetic simplicity and are the work of talented people; but they are always somewhat imitative, grotesquely echoing Baroque or the Neo-classic artists.

Orneore Metelli, a shoemaker of Terni, was no doubt the first important naïve painter in Italy. It is said that, after his long day's work, he spent his nights bent over a kitchen table, painting his sublime scenes of everyday life with colors mixed in coffee cups. He had no easel and no studio, but his inner vision kept him working until dawn.

In his *Procession in Front of Terni Cathedral* (page 248), we see priests carrying banners and

Adolf Dietrich: Zoo

crosses through the cold stone architecture of the provincial town. Everything is well ordered, as we might expect of a craftsman. The people line the streets; the policemen in their black uniforms and shiny hats seem larger than life. Just as well ordered and classical in feeling is Metelli's view of the Piazza Vittore Emmanuele in Terni (page 249) with the statue of a figure in a white toga, standing before a

133

classical arcade—columns, domes, battlements, and sculptures on the roofs. The ghostly emptiness of the square recalls Chirico. We are close to the rhetorical. In Latin American naïve art the Spanish heritage and folklore have survived in the costumes, hats, woven fabrics, and in the architecture; in Italy the great political and cultural past and the impressive architecture of the cities have made their way into naïve painting.

Such is the setting for many of Metelli's scenes of processions and celebrations (colorplate, page 135; page 250). He has also depicted interior scenes, a confessional, for example, and opera performances. But everywhere we feel the presence of local and regional folklore elements. His native Terni had an orchestra that gave public concerts, and Metelli belonged to it. The orchestra, like the fire brigade, was a feature of civic life; at all events, the members of the orchestra wore uniforms, too. Metelli painted himself in this costume—black coat with plenty of gold braid and, embroidered on the sleeve, a lyre symbolizing the sublimity of music. He is shown leaning against a chair, which is as green as the feathers in his hat, and stares fixedly—prominent nose by no means understated, small bright red mouth partly concealed by a rakish mustache. Every-

thing about this self-portrait is serious and solemn. The naïve painter is fully conscious of his own importance; musicians are among the notables of Terni.

Rosina Viva was a refugee in Switzerland during the Second World War, when she began to paint out of homesickness. Her delicately embroidered artificial flowers look toward the window from their dainty vases. The Gulf of Naples, shaped like an open hand, is the paradise of her dreams. Brilliant colors illumine the sea, and we are not surprised to find Mount Vesuvius and the island of Capri, where the painter was born.

She paints melancholy picture-post-card scenes, recollections of childhood, daydreams in front of a little mirror on the wall, and fishermen. Her frequently mentioned *Wedding at the Foot of Vesuvius* (page 247) shows a dark-eyed bride with veil and bouquet, and a bridegroom standing stiffly with white gloves and a black suit. In the back, we see the parents and a little dog. The grass is sprouting between the paving stones in front of the white church. In the background is the symbolic brown-and-violet volcano, quiescent now, however, in honor of the occasion. The picture captures a mood,

Orneore Metelli: My Departure for Military Service

as a popular song does—a sweet, somewhat sentimental Neapolitan song—and yet it is not unmoving in its innocence.

The pharmacist Bernardo Pasotti, a native of Milan, is too busy to paint very often. He constructs his landscapes and views of cities in fluid colors and lively rhythms, with a flair for composition. In *Cathedral of Cremona* (page 251) there are no living human figures; the stone sculptures on the roof of the arcade and in the niches and medallions serve as actors in this architectural drama. Pasotti displays none of the pedantry of the pharmaceutical profession in his art. He does not draw stone by stone, as do many naïve painters, but is fascinated by the spirit of a monument, by the structure of a cathedral. Geometric forms, rosettes, columns, pediments, and portals serve him as elements in a deliberately organized fugal composition. Like the German painter Paps, Pasotti is a sensitive artist who instinctively controls his material, but his works are not always naïve in the strict sense.

Cesare Breveglieri was originally from Milan, and was a teacher, a clerk, and a traveling salesman. As a boy, he wanted to be a painter, but his father urged him to take up some more profitable trade. His mother, a very pious woman, regarded art as sinful. "In her thoughts she saw me wallowing in sin with naked models," he says. So he let himself be sidetracked. Like many other self-taught artists, he painted after his working day ended. His paintings attracted attention. He received support and prizes, and finally went to Paris. Rousseau and Utrillo influenced him. The Sunday painter developed into a naïve painter by conscious choice. What he observes, he renders in vigorous colors, and in his paintings, too, architecture plays a considerable role. His interiors and his own studio with nude models, like his scenes of hunting, horse races, streets, and parks, exhibit a somewhat awkward Fauvism, conscious observation, and critical formulation. He, too, is an example of the borderline primitive.

A few talented Italian painters deliberately turned away from the bravura and rhetoric of the *novecènto* and took the path of naïve Surrealism or of the candid realism of the *maîtres populaires*. More vigorous and intense than the German Georgy Stefula, Ottone Rosai captured the poetic sadness of the poor quarters in Florence in paintings that reveal austere simplification and naïve emotion. Renouncing all coloristic effects and skilled draftsmanship, he deliberately moved toward a robust realism that derives from the Douanier Rousseau.

Giuseppe Cesetti, who began as a self-taught painter, is one of the consciously naïve artists who seek to go beyond rationalism and achieve a primitive poetry. His pastoral scenes and his other landscapes tend toward emblematic simplification. He achieves this result, however, which sometimes borders on the decorative, by drawing not upon primitive and archaic motifs, but upon literary reminiscences.

Antonio Donghi, Umberto Lillani, and Domenico Cantatore, all of whom have probably been influenced both by Rousseau's magic and the austere idiom of the Neo-primitives, cannot be regarded as naïve painters, but they may be mentioned as examples of the attempt to reinvigorate traditional, sophisticated art through drawing upon the subterranean springs of primitive spontaneity.

The irruption of archaic and primitive elements into modern art could be illustrated by other examples—for instance, the works of the Mexican artists Rivera, Orozco, and Tamayo. The Yugoslav group *Zemlia* also sought to rejuvenate the traditional by drawing upon peasant art. Krsto Hegedušić has combined archaic symbols with Surrealist techniques. Max Beckmann went all the way back to prehistoric art. Fernand Léger, who was a friend of the Douanier, painted his machinelike creatures striding like dinosaurs across the twentieth century in the monumental style of the "greater reality." Utrillo's soundless wailing walls built of mortar and white zinc are in keeping with the naïve definition of reality. But his candor falls inside, rather than outside, the rich heritage of Impressionism. The humility and naïve humanity of his works also reflect the sophisticated sensibility of more highly developed art.

In Belgium and in the Netherlands, the term "primitive" first of all suggests medieval painting. But the tragic quality, the introspective faces, the sharp realism, and the Gothic sense of mystery have rarely been echoed by the Neo-primitives of these countries. Louis Delattre, who was born in Ghent in 1815, may have been an exception. He had an eccentric, restless career, becoming a mechanic, house painter, banker, photographer, and artist. In 1865 he experimented with a flying machine of his own invention, but without success. His fellow citizens called him "the flying man." His paintings reveal an original imagination. *The Birth of the World* and *Friday Market* have been lost; the *Ascension of Prince Baudouin* (page 252) attracted attention at the exhibition of naïve art at Knokke in 1958.

We are tempted to ask whether Delattre was guided by an ironic intention when, in 1891, he painted this obscure gathering of the highest European dignitaries and God's heavenly envoys. The group of mourners is shown standing around a rather ugly tomb, from which the dead prince in his full-dress uniform is being carried by pink cupids on a rather gay ascension to heaven. Possibly this picture seems odd only to the viewer of today. Delattre may have painted a genre scene of mourning in the popular taste. The Surrealist combination of realistic and supernatural elements, and the photographic accuracy in depicting fantastic events, reflect a primitive conception that produces an effect of strangeness which is surely not intentional.

Léon Greffe, born at Charleroi in 1881, was a miner who left Belgium to work in the Paris food markets (Les Halles); later, he was a concierge. From an attic of the building that he served, he painted the Paris quais, the Palais de Justice, the Pont Neuf, and other views and compositions. The freshness and forcefulness that characterize his *Pont Neuf* also characterize his *Bastille Day in a Small Town* (page 253), which he painted from memory. This has been a favorite subject with many naïve painters. Dancing and music are invariably depicted. Léon Greffe possesses a strong feeling for the language of color. His human figures and houses are as cheerful as in children's drawings. We are shown folk dancing on a golden ocher ground and, in the foreground, townspeople in their Sunday black strolling on the green grass.

Camille van Hyfte, born at Ertvelde in 1886, was a farmer; later, he owned a slaughterhouse for horses in a Paris suburb; and, still later, he rode in bicycle races. Jakovsky praises him for his strong sense of atmosphere, his deep slate-colored skies, and his representations of country fairs and of the many-colored façades of Belgian houses. His interiors evoke a mysterious, old-fashioned world in sober brush strokes. His *Interior with Flowers* (color-plate, page 141), painted in 1951, shows a greatly foreshortened room with green and wine-red wallpaper. It is almost empty—there are four chairs, and two tables, on one of which stands a monumental vase with flowers in thickly applied ivory, sepia, and black colors. The disproportions among the things and the unexpectedness of the colors give this work a peculiar charm. It is as though something else were present in the room, something that we cannot quite discern.

Micheline Boyadjian was born at Bruges in 1923. Her very un-French last name is that of her husband, a native of Georgia in Caucasia. One of her paintings, *The Umbrellas* (page 252), represents a street during a rain. The colors are bright and attractive, and the scene has been caught in a carefree manner; the work is naïve in the way in which the story is told rather than in its artistic conception. The opened umbrellas are like so many ornamental domes or knobs. The picturesque people carrying them are drawn in profile or in rigorous front view, as they take mincing steps to avoid the puddles. We are reminded of a nursery rhyme by Christian Morgenstern:

Spann dein kleines Schirmchen auf,
denn es möchte regnen drauf.

[Open up your little umbrella,
the rain might want to fall on it.]

Edgar Tytgat's poetic legends are refined in their naïveté. His ever-so-slightly melancholy scenes of country fairs, with sad, graceful clowns and pairs of lovers—like his solemn religious processions—seem to have been taken from popular illustrated books. They are close to the childish heart of life. But behind the candid, colorful scenes from puppet shows, with their peasantlike decor, there is the expert sense of artistic form that we might expect of a superior stage director.

Jan van Weert, a Dutchman born at s'Hertogenbosch, has been a travel agent, a horse breeder, and a jockey. He now lives at Düsseldorf. He began to paint in his seventies, after the Second World War, "out of boredom, because I had nothing else to do." He likes to paint the streets and canals of Amsterdam; other subjects are windmills, sleigh rides, and men on horseback—all drawn from his own recollections. His work has qualities of directness and candor, and is permeated with the gentle romanticism of old age.

Sipke Cornelis Houtman, a baker in Amsterdam, began to paint at the age of sixty. His self-portrait discloses a gift for candid observation, a delicate sensibility, and an awkward technique. His picture of birds in a cage (page 255) is perhaps meant as an allegory: the beauty in man is imprisoned until the artist releases it. His *Garden in the Amsterdam Home for the Aged*, rendered almost two-dimensionally, is like an intricate geometric ornament.

Sal Meijer, a Dutch diamond cutter, paints the canals and the lacy stonework of Amsterdam. The bricks of the houses glitter; the cool green light of the early morning shimmers like flower petals in a gentle breeze from the sea. His placid cows seem held in an aquarium of time. Loyalty shines out of their beady black eyes as they chew their cud. This naïve painter places his cows in a row, much as the old masters arranged their group portraits of municipal corporations and guilds. He wants us really to appreciate all of them. Some of them look directly at us with friendly eyes. Though these are not sacred animals, they are man's useful helpmates, and the painter loves them, perhaps because they are so patient.

Whereas, in the United States, amateur painting developed independently of the academies, it was a pursuit of cultivated art lovers in England. Aristocratic young ladies, members of the government, and prosperous businessmen produced poetic watercolors, landscapes, flowers, and, occasionally, animals and portraits, which are often characterized by refined taste and sense of form. The Institute for Contemporary Art in London gives exhibitions of these well-bred works, which are painted by men and women for whom art is a hobby, and which reflect the cheerfulness and relaxation of people who go fishing on their holidays. It was only when artists and art lovers alike became aware of art as independent of tradition and the schools—as a direct expression of the creative instinct—that it was realized that England, too, has had her naïve painters among people of humble origin.

Alfred Wallis, a fisherman and storekeeper born at Devonport, was discovered by Ben Nicolson and Christopher Wood. Bold drawing and subtle color characterize his works. The type of perspective

that he used in *The Bridge* (page 259) recalls Egyptian reliefs. It shows a kind of viaduct in a night landscape, and the narrow line of a train appears at the upper edge. In the background loom black trees bathed in an unreal, misty light. There are shimmering gray walls, and whitish shadows that suggest human figures. On the murky, light-green water ships are sailing or lie at anchor. The picture has a ghostly quality. The few crudely drawn lines of the slanting piers and the arches of the bridge suggest the harshness and robustness of the life of English fishermen and sailors.

Scottie Wilson, born into a Glasgow working-class family, frequently appears in exhibitions of naïve painters. His calligraphic visions, which recall the abstract, subterranean realms of Paul Klee, are, however, more fantastic than naïve. The naïve painters are closely linked with reality: it was naïve art that rediscovered the object. But Scottie Wilson, in such pictures as *Quiet Village in the Mountains* (page 258), cuts the umbilical cord that links us to the visual appearance of things.

Lack of training does not necessarily imply naïveté. Many important professional painters began as self-taught amateurs. In the last analysis, every artist is his own teacher. Hard work can transform a tyro into a master. But naïve art stops at the point where the painter has tasted of the fruits of formal knowledge. Once the artist becomes aware of the distinction between the idea of the object and the object itself, he ceases to be direct and intuitive, and becomes reflective. For, as Kant long ago pointed out, naïveté is simply the eruption of sincerity originally natural to mankind, not to be confused with the disguises with which sophisticated artists overlay visual appearances, as a kind of second nature.

The vital strength of peasant and primitive painters is that they have not been touched by such knowledge. Because they are untrained, self-directed, they can create spontaneously out of inner impulse or need.

The Polish painter Nikifor of Krynica, who has forgotten his family name and never knew his mother (she was a professional beggar), had a speech defect and communicated with his surroundings by means of the paintbrush. The written characters of his visual vocabulary are screeching semaphores, bridges gone wild, street wildly careening (page 260).

He has also portrayed saints with fur caps. He often portrays himself as a scholar interpreting the Scriptures. This is how the naïve painter compensates for his ignorance, by giving himself the role of a sage on earth and a place next to the saints in heaven. An instinctive storyteller, he eliminates rational causality and transforms the familiar world. In a Polish biography of Nikifor, we read: "He is not a Sunday painter because he paints every day. He is not an amateur, because he treats his art with extraordinary seriousness (after all he lives by it), and yet he is at the same time a true primitive artist."

Another Polish painter, Teofil Ociepka, born in 1893, is a miner. In his spare time he paints the fantastic landscapes of prehistory as he imagines it. His virgin forests are more than natural wildernesses. Beasts, both real and imaginary, pursue and exterminate one another. In soft, flaky colors, like those of peasant blankets, he tells of terrors. Perhaps these were the visions seen deep underground in the mines. His saturnine monsters have big sad eyes, and masklike faces almost human in feeling, partly hidden by gigantic beaks. One of his paintings shows an enormous animal strangling a tiny mouse with its trunk.

Farther east we find the Georgian primitive artist Niko Pirosmanoshvili. He wanted to paint as a boy, but instead he was sent to work on the railroads, and, by this means, he traveled back and forth across the vast expanses of Russia. In his spare time, he painted signs for inns and pictures for himself. He never studied in any school, but he was obviously influenced by Georgian frescoes. He painted on oilcloth, tin, and cardboard. At first his pictures were light in color, but later he applied shrill greens, blues, and yellows on a black ground. Among his favorite subjects are scenes from the life of his people—holiday celebrations and banquets (pages 261–63). Occasionally he takes subjects from orally transmitted folk legends.

The closer we have come to Asia, the harder it has been to keep a sharp distinction between folk art and more highly developed art, for all the art in these regions is deeply rooted in tradition and has scarcely become aware of itself in the self-conscious way of the West.

Dit l'Etranger parmi les sables, "toute chose m'est nouvelle!..."
Et la naissance du chant ne lui est pas moins étrangère.

Saint-John Perse, Exil, *1942*

[Says the Stranger on the sands, "the whole world is new to me!..."
And the birth of his song is no less alien to him.]

Tr. Denis Devlin, Pantheon Books, New York, 1949

X Return to Nature

Anyone brought up on traditional art history, in the course of a conventional education, may, naturally, find himself somewhat at sea in dealing with the modern primitives. The very concept of modern primitivism is hard to define, and the topic spills over into psychology, psychiatry, and comparative anthropology. In a sense, what we have been calling "naïve" art is still largely uncharted territory, and the customary intellectual credentials scarcely suffice for the purpose of a passport. Today, when our sense not only of style but of cultural unity in general is in disintegration, and firmly established, traditional norms no longer exist, it is becoming possible to identify with a more "primitive" situation existing prior to the establishment of order and conscious continuity. Modern man, in his art, has turned back to myth precisely because his newly attained dominion over nature has become a weapon against life, precisely because the triumph of technology has been accomplished at the price of spiritual impoverishment. These developments are reflected in art today, both by the new interest in the art of archaic epochs and by the development of a neo-primitive art itself.

Half a century ago, nobody had ever heard the term "naïve art" or "art of the naïve." Henri Rousseau, a man who seemed grotesque to his contemporaries—an eccentric, a clown—was its first and greatest prophet. The other artists of his day were alternately amused and fascinated by him.

It might be interesting to ask whether there are historic precedents for our present interest in the primitive, our appreciation of the naïve. This interest may be symptomatic of that stage in the life of a culture when nature is no longer directly experienced, but known only through the intermediary of philosophy or art. When the shepherd's flute no longer serves to call the flocks, it can serve as symbol to evoke a golden past in art and literature.

Although doubtless important in itself as a defense of life against the alienation from nature that civili-zation brings with it, the desire to go back to a lost simplicity, the idea of a *return* to nature, has often been little more than a theme of sophisticated conversation, a fashionable topic, a kind of artistic game.

Under the New Kingdom of ancient Egypt, the lovers we find portrayed as simple, "natural" boys and girls were the creations of court poets. Similarly, the Idylls of Theocritus evoke archaic scenes, but the poet's folk manner is the product of the most refined poetic skill. The Hellenistic pastoral novels, and the bucolic poetry of the Augustans can be understood only as reflections of weariness with urban overcivilization. The pastoral poems, novels, and plays of Italian and Spanish origin seem to have been expressing a cult of "return to nature" under feudalism. During the Rococo period and the Enlightenment, pastoral themes once again served—even in stage design—to reawaken a new sensibility, also imbued with feeling for "nature" as opposed to urban society. It is characteristic of all these movements invoking the past as a Golden Age of simplicity and naturalness—from classical antiquity down to Jean Jacques Rousseau—that they invariably arose within highly developed, secure civilizations. It is overabundance that makes simplicity attractive, excessive wealth and luxury that make people want to be "natural" again. Only over the past century has "the common man" as such become a theme of art. Walt Whitman heralded this development:

I advance from the people in their own spirit,
Here is what sings unrestricted faith.
Song of Myself

By a curious historical coincidence, it is possible to trace the three latest stages in this development of a "return to nature" by invoking the names of three men called Rousseau.

The first of these, Jean Jacques, taught that culture is authentic only insofar as it embodies nature at a higher level of development.

Théodore, the second, left Paris and set up his easel outdoors in the woods and fields near Barbizon. He lived in a barn, and, by the example of his deep feeling for nature in his life and works, gave inspiration to the subsequent development of *plein-air* painting.

Henri Rousseau, it is quite possible, may never have heard of his illustrious namesakes. Such is the opinion of the critic Roger-Marx, in any event. Rousseau was not an educated man, nor did he read

a great deal for self-education. He rarely left the city of Paris. Nonetheless, his deep sense of affinity and communion with nature is the most remarkable quality of his art. In an age of alienation—the alienation of man from nature, of man from things—this third Rousseau brought the gift of the "greater reality," the prophecy of a new harmony between man and things, between the self and the world.

It was Henri Rousseau who painted the Angel of Freedom, calling the artists of France with the wine-red trumpet of hope to come and exhibit at the twenty-second Salon des Indépendants. But it is really Henri Rousseau himself who has turned out to be the guardian angel of twentieth-century art.

I can imagine him in this role today, summoning the naïve artists of all nations and continents to come together and constitute one great exhibition of modern primitive painting—without interference from juries and with only the purest, most sincere expressions of artistic creativeness. It is not difficult to visualize him, his earnest eyes glowing beneath his artist's beret, receiving the long procession of his followers and descendants. Many of them have come very far to be here, to present their homage to the master, in the form of paintings rolled under their arms or carried in frames. Some have brought canvases so enormous that carts and wagons alone can hold them.

Leaning on his cane, the aged post-office inspector, Vivin, is at the head of the line. He, the builder of cities, has brought an example of his work in which the cobweb of his lines has imprisoned with abstract rhythm the streets and squares of Paris.

Slight and stooped, eyes burning in her pale face, Séraphine is next, with her mystic, ecstatic, shimmering painting of flowers.

The tall, thin man with the pointed beard, who stands so stiffly, is André Bauchant. He has brought with him an epic tribute to his admired ancients— perhaps to Homer, Pericles, Neptune, or Cleopatra.

Camille Bombois is next, with his wrestlers and weight lifters, his clowns and enormous women in pink tights.

At once shy and coquettish, the old man with the glasses is Morris Hirshfield, who has under his arm yet another of his naked, tailor-made beauties—those old men's darlings.

José Guadalupe Posada has come all the way from Mexico with his *calavera* of bicycles ridden by skeletons in some six-day version of the Dance of Death.

The voodoo priest, Hector Hyppolite, is surrounded by friends and pupils, and all have examples of their warm, exotic retellings of ancient legends.

John Kane is in from Pittsburgh, with dreary loft and office buildings preserved forever in the work that he has brought with him. Thorvald Arenst Hoyer is with him, with a dewy scene of the Kentucky mountains.

And there is Thomas Chambers, with one of his pictures of Niagara Falls under his arm, the rushing spray like a shimmering curtain of nylon. Grandma Moses is right in line, her picture sparkling with the melting snows of a rural March. Adolf Dietrich has brought a landscape of the gently rolling hills around Lake Constance, his own serenity reflected in the silky blue surface of the water.

Next comes a small Yugoslav delegation, led by Ivan Generalić, the painter of Hlebine. He and his disciples have preserved for posterity the bright green meadows of summer, the white of the cloaks that the shepherds wear in winter, and the golden cinnabar of the Balkan autumn.

Dominique Lagru, coal miner and herdsman, has brought one of his alarming representations of the monsters of prehistory, a picture that will have to be hung far away from the one Edward Hicks has with him of a chubby infant nuzzled by lions and jackals in peaceable harmony with sheep and cows.

Ah, good! Aloys Sauter has brought his wife, the poetess, along. She is wearing her best black lace dress and at any moment now will recite the ode she has written to world peace. It will be hard to hear above the hubbub of the World Exhibition, for it seems that some of the infants portrayed by the early American limners are about to cry, and the carriage in O'Brady's street scene of old Montmartre is clattering over the cobblestones, while Morill's saucy banjo player is plunking away and Joseph Pickett's early locomotive chug-chugs along under a fearful head of steam.

Not everyone has arrived yet, but there is still room for the late-comers, as well as for primitive painters in countries that we have never visited, or wherever they are, who have not as yet revealed themselves, to their contemporaries.

The Polish peasant painter Nikifor, in his heavy fur cap, is in a playful mood—he unpins the star that he is wearing and inserts it in the sky of Felicindo Acevedo's picture, which symbolically brings Christopher Columbus back to us from the New World. And there is Theora Hamblett, with one of her glaring yellow visions, quite sufficient of itself to serve as flash bulb for the photographers who will surely not miss this opening.

These painters bring us the revelation that myth has not departed altogether from our science-dominated, industrialized world. Somewhere in the middle distance of our lives—equidistant from the microscopic and the telescopic poles of our more pretentious concerns—stand these homely, authentic painters and their images of a human spirit that has not, after all, lost contact with art's primordial origins.

Acknowledgments

The idea for this book first came to me many years ago, in the between-wars period, when I met Wilhelm Uhde. After I had published a study of the Yugoslav painters, some years later, this project took definite form. The writing of this book was made possible by the exhibition "La peinture naïve du Douanier Rousseau à nos jours" at Knokke-le-Zoute, Belgiums, which I helped to organize.

I should like to express my thanks also to M. Émile Langui, general director of the Fine Arts in Belgium; M. Bert Urvater, member of the Commission for the Royal Museums of Fine Arts in Belgium; and M. P. G. van Hecke, who assembled examples of the work of naïve painters all over the world on the walls of the Casino at Knokke.

The book has profited from valuable suggestions in conversations with M. Jean Cassou, director of the Musée National de l'Art Moderne in Paris; with Dr. Kurt Martin, general director of the Bavarian State Galleries, Munich; and with the painter Krsto Hegedušić, the initiator of the School of Hlebine. I also wish to thank M. Anatole Jakovsky, with whom I had a fruitful exchange of letters.

It is today scarcely possible to study the primitive art of our time without knowing the works of Mr. Alfred H. Barr, Jr., director of the Museum of Modern Art in New York; Mr. Robert Goldwater, director of the Museum of Primitive Art in New York; and Mr. Sidney Janis, the well-known dealer and collector, of New York.

I do not want to forget to mention here the collaboration of my wife, Lise Bihalji, who shared in every stage of my labors. For suggestions and photographs, author and publisher alike are indebted to Mr. George Staempfli, who organized the exhibition in the American pavilion of the Brussels World Fair in 1958; Mr. José Gómez-Sicre, chief of the Visual Art section of the Pan-American Union, Washington; Mr. Thomas Grochowiak, who was in charge of the exhibition "From Rousseau to the Miners of the Ruhr," held in connection with the 12th Ruhrfestspiele at Recklinghausen; the Kunstsalon Wolfsberg in Zurich; and the Gallery of Primitive Art in Zagreb.

OTO BIHALJI-MERIN

Bibliography

Chapters I-IV

Broch, Hermann. Essay "Hugo von Hofmannsthal und seine Zeit," in *Dichten und Erkennen.* Zurich: Rheinverlag, 1955.

Cassou, Jean. "Les maîtres populaires de la réalité," *Art Vivant* (Paris) No. 214 (August-September, 1937).

————. *Situation de l'Art Moderne.* Paris: Editions de Minuit, 1950.

Ehlers, Otto August. *Sonntagsmaler.* With the collaboration of Bernhard Jasmand and Otto Kallir. Berlin-Darmstadt: Verlag Ehlers, 1956.

Francastel, Pierre. *Art et technique.* Paris: Editions de Minuit, 1956.

Gauguin, Paul. *Avant et après.* Paris: G. Crès et Cie., 1923.

Geist, Hans Friedrich. "Der Malunterricht an Volksschulen," *Graphis* (Zurich), No. 77 (1958).

Guenne, Jacques. "La naïveté est-elle un art?" *Art Vivant* (Paris) No. 147 (April 1931).

Haftmann, Werner. *Malerei im zwanzigsten Jahrhundert.* Munich: Prestel Verlag, 1957.

Halbwachs, M. "La mémoire collective et le temps," in *Cahiers Internationaux de Sociologie* (Paris: Ecole pratique des hautes études), 1947.

Huyghe, René. "La peinture d'instinct." Introduction to *Histoire de l'art contemporain: La peinture.* Paris: Alcan, 1935.

Jakovsky, Anatole. "Ces peintres de la semaine de sept dimanches." Preface to catalogue of exhibition "La peinture naïve du douanier Rousseau à nos jours," Knokke-le-Zoute, Belgium, 1958.

Jung, Carl Gustav. *Bewusstes und Unbewusstes.* Frankfurt am Main: Fischer Verlag, 1957.

Kandinsky, Wassily. "Über die Formfrage," in *Blauer Reiter.* Munich, 1912. Reprinted in *Essays über Kunst und Künstler,* ed. Max Bill. Stuttgart, 1955.

Keller, Dieter. *Eine Sammlung alter Hinterglasbilder.* Published by the author, Stuttgart, no date.

Kriss, Rettenbeck; Lenz. *Das Votivbild.* Verlag Hermann Rinn, 1958.

Lhote, André. "Art populaire," *Nouvelle Revue Française* (Paris: August, 1929).

Malraux, André. *The Psychology of Art.* New York: Pantheon Books, 1949–50.

Meyer, Franz. "Primitive im zwanzigsten Jahrhundert," *Du* (Zurich), No. 2 (February, 1952).

Michailov, Nikola. "Zur Begriffsbestimmung der Laienmalerei," *Zeitschrift für Kunstgeschichte,* (Berlin) No. 5–6 (1935).

Prinzhorn, H. *Bildnerei der Geisteskranken.* Berlin: J. Springer, 1923.

Read, Herbert. *Art and Society.* London: Faber & Faber, 1956.

————. *The Philosophy of Modern Art.* New York: Meridian Books, 1955.

Roh, Juliane. *Ich habe wunderbare Hilf erlangt.* Munich: Bruckmann Verlag, 1957.

Sydow, Eckart von. *Primitive Kunst und Psychoanalyse.* Leipzig: Internationaler Psychoanalytischer Verlag, 1927. Imagobücher X.

Tomlinson, R. R. *Children as Artists.* London, New York: King Penguin Books, 1944.

Chapter V

Basler, Adolphe. *Henri Rousseau.* Paris: Librairie de France, 1927.

Cooper, Douglas. *Henri Rousseau.* Paris: Braun & Cie, 1951.

Courthion, Pierre. *Henri Rousseau.* Geneva: Skira, 1944.

Gauthier, Maximilien. *Henri Rousseau.* Paris: Ed. Les Gémeaux, 1949.

Perruchot, Henri. *Le douanier Rousseau.* Paris: Ed. Universitaires, 1957.

Rich, Daniel Catton. *Henri Rousseau.* New York: Museum of Modern Art, 1942.

Salmon, A. *Henri Rousseau, dit le douanier.* Paris: Editions Crès, 1927.

Soupault, Philippe. *Henri Rousseau, le douanier.* Paris: Editions des Quatre Chemins, 1927.

Uhde, Wilhelm. *Henri Rousseau, le douanier.* Paris: Ed. Figuière, 1911.

Uhde, Wilhelm. *Henri Rousseau*. Bern: Alfred Scherz Verlag, 1948.
———. *Henri Rousseau*. Düsseldorf: Flechtheim Verlag, 1914.
Werner, Alfred. *Henri Rousseau*. New York: Harry N. Abrams Inc., 1957.

Chapter VI

Bing-Bodmer, Henri. "Lettre sur Louis Vivin," *Du* (Zurich), No. 2 (February, 1952).
———. *Camille Bombois*. Paris: Ed. de la Galerie Bing, 1951.
Gauthier, Maximilien. *André Bauchant*. Paris: Ed. du Chêne, 1943.
———. *Jean Eve*. Paris: Ed. Les Gémeaux, 1950.
Georges, Waldemar. "Populisme ou romanisme: André Bauchant," *Formes* (Paris) No. 15 (February, 1931).
Jakovsky, Anatole. *Louis Vivin, peintre de Paris*. Paris: Ed. Jacques Damase, 1951.
———. *Les Peintres Naïfs*. Paris: Bibl. des Arts, 1956.
———. *La Peinture naïve*. Paris: Ed. Damase, 1949.
———. *Die naive Malerei in Frankreich*. Introduction by Florent Fels. Zurich: Diogenes Verlag, 1947.
Uhde, Wilhelm. *Five Primitive Masters*. Translated by Ralph Thompson from the German edition of 1947. New York: Quadrangle Press, 1949.

Chapter VII

Cahill, Holger. *American Folk Art 1750–1900*. New York: The Museum of Modern Art, 1932.
Cheek, Leslie, Jr. Preface to catalogue of exhibition "American Folk Art" in American Pavilion of Brussels World's Fair, 1958.
Ford, Alice. *Pictorial Folk Art, New England to California*. New York and London: Studio Publications, Inc., 1949.
Janis, Sidney. *They Taught Themselves. American Primitive Painters of the 20th Century*. Preface by Alfred H. Barr, Jr. New York: Dial Press, 1942.

Lipman, Jean. *American Primitive Painting*. London, New York, Toronto: Oxford University Press, 1942.
Lipman, Jean, and Winchester, Alice. *Primitive Painters in America, 1750–1950*. New York: Dodd Mead & Co., 1950.
Masters of Popular Painting. Modern Primitives of Europe and America. Texts by Holger Cahill, Maximilien Gauthier, Jean Cassou, Dorothy C. Miller, et al. New York: Museum of Modern Art, 1938.
Morvan, Pierre. "Aufbruch der Kunst," *Du* (Zurich: September, 1958).
Moses, Anna Mary Robertson (Grandma Moses). *My Life's History*. Edited by Otto Kallir. New York: Harper & Brothers, 1951.
Posada. *Las Obras de José Guadalupe Posada, grabador mexicano*. Edited by Frances Toor, Paul O. Higgins, and Blas Vanegas Arroyo. Mexico, 1930.
Rodman, Selden. *Horace Pippin: A Negro Painter in America*. New York: University Place Book Shop, 1946.
———. *Renaissance in Haiti*. New York: Pellegrini and Cudahy, 1948.
———. *Haiti, the Black Republic*. New York: Devin Adair, 1954.
Roh, Franz. "Haiti-Maler und die kulturelle Rückströmung," *Die Kunst und das schöne Heim*, (Munich: F. Bruckmann) Vol. 49, No. 12 (September, 1951).

Chapter VIII

Basicević, Micá. Preface to catalogue of exhibition "Les Primitifs yougoslaves," Dubrovnik, 1956. Reprinted in German and English in *Yugoslavia* (Belgrade) No. 14 (1958).
Bek, Božidar. "L'Ecole de Hlebine." Preface to catalogue of exhibition of Yugoslav Primitives, São Paulo, 1955.
Bihalji-Merin, Oto. *The Art of the Naïve Painters of Yugoslavia*. With the collaboration of Mirjana Gvozdanović and Siniša Paunović. Belgrade: Verlag Jugoslavij, 1958.
Gvozdanović, Mirjana. "Eugen Buktenica." Preface to catalogue of exhibition of Dalmatian fishermen painters, Gallery of Primitive Art, Zagreb, 1957.

Chapter IX

Bigiaretti, Libero. *Orneore Metelli*. Ivrea: Centro Cultur. Olivetti, 1957.

Breton André. Preface to catalogue of exhibition at Galerie Mirador, Paris, 1950 (on works of G. Vivancos).

Courthion, Pierre. Preface to monograph on Metelli. Edited by P. Cailler. Geneva, 1951.

Gasser, Hans Ulrich. "Appenzeller Bauernmalerei," *Graphis* (Zurich), No. 69 (January-February, 1957).

Gasser, Manuel. "Adolf Dietrich," *Du* (Zurich: January, 1958).

Hoenn, C. *Adolf Dietrich*. Frauenfeld: Verlag Huber, 1942.

Poensgen, Georg. *Ringelnatz als Maler*. Berlin: K. Henssel Verlag, 1958.

Ries, Margot. "Der Maler Dietrich," in *Kunst für alle*, 1927.

Roh, Franz. "Oluf Braren, einsamer Laienmaler auf der Insel Föhr," in *Das Kunstwerk*, No. 5–6 (November-December, 1957).

Valsecchi, Marco. *La pittura di Rosina Viva*. Milan: Ediz. del Milione, 1953.

Additional Illustrations

Bildtafeln

1　Henri Rousseau　France

2　Henri Rousseau　France

3 Henri Rousseau France

4 Henri Rousseau France

161

5   Henri Rousseau   France

6   Henri Rousseau   France

163

7 Louis Vivin France

8 Louis Vivin France

9 Camille Bombois   France

10 Camille Bombois   France

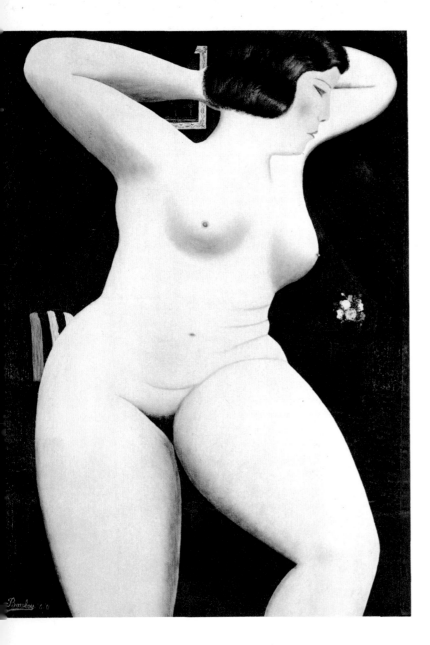

168

11 Camille Bombois France   12 Séraphine (Séraphine Louis) France

13 André Bauchant France

14 André Bauchant France

15 André Bauchant France

16 Emile Blondel France

17 Dominique Lagru France

21 Louis Augustin Déchelette   France

22 Louis Augustin Déchelette   France

23 André Bouquet   France

24 René Rimbert France

25 O'Brady (G. Mac Brady) Franc

27 O'Brady (G. Mac Brady) France   26 O'Brady (G. Mac Brady) France

28 Jean Fous France
29 Jean Fous France
30 Jean Fous France
31 Jean Fous France

32 Aloys Sauter France

33 Aloys Sauter France

185

34 F. Boilauges France

35 André Demonchy France

37 Benjamin Parker   USA

38 Edward Hicks   USA

39 Edward Hicks   USA

40 Linton Park USA

41 Linton Park USA

42 Joseph Pickett   USA

43 Joseph Pickett   USA

44　Joseph Becker　USA

45 D. Morrill USA

198   46 Edwin Romanzo Elmer   USA   47 Edwin Romanzo Elmer   USA

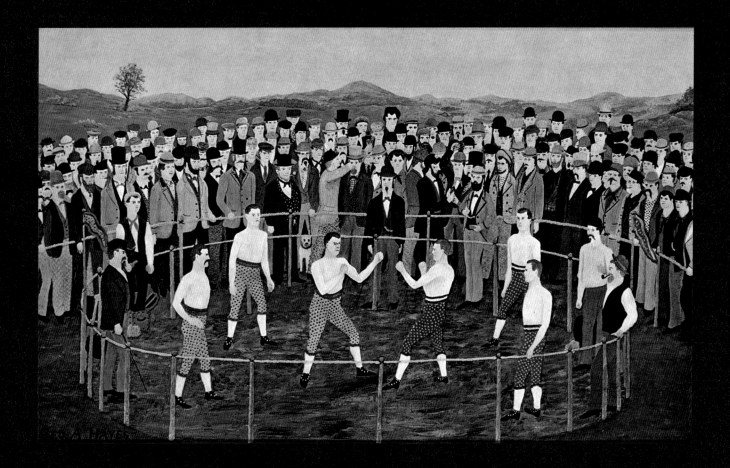

49a Horace Pippin USA

49b Horace Pippin USA

204

50   John Kane   USA

51   John Kane   USA

52 Morris Hirshfield USA

53 Morris Hirshfield USA

54 Morris Hirshfield   USA

55 Morris Hirshfield   USA

56　Théora Hamblett　USA

57　Patrick J. Sullivan　USA

58　Streeter Blair　USA

60c Isreal Litvak USA   60d Lawrence H. Lebduska USA

61 Rigaud Benoit   Haïti

62 Enguérrand Gourgue   Haïti

63 Wilson Bigaud   Haïti

64 Philomé Obin Haïti

Gesnerr Abelard   Haïti

66   Hector Hyppolite   Haïti

219

220

67   Antonio J. Velazquez   España

68   Antonio J. Velazquez   España

222

69 Yvan Généralic Jugoslavija

70 Eugen Buktenica Jugoslavija

71 Yvan Généralic Jugoslavija

72 Mijo Kovačić Jugoslavija

73 Vangel Naumovski   Jugoslavija

74 Eugen Buktenica   Jugoslavija

75 Franjo Filipović   Jugoslavija

76 Janko Brašić Jugoslavija

77 Ivan Večenaj Jugoslavija   229

78 Janko Brašić Jugoslavija

79 Jano Knjazović Jugoslavija

80 Jano Sokol Jugoslavija

81 Mirko Virius Jugoslavija

82 Cvetan Belić Jugoslavija

83 Emerik Fejes Jugoslavija

84 Votivbild

Durch die Anrufung Maria
ist geholfen worden. 1882

86 Oluf Braren Deutschland

Zieh sich ein yeyts selbst bey Der nasn
Waß dich ni Frendt Thue auch nicht Blasn.

88 Unbekannter Bergmann Deutschland

89 Christian Thegen Deutschland

90 Adalbert Trillhaase Deutschland

91 Joachim Ringelnatz Deutschland

242

92 Ramholz (Felix Muche)
Deutschland

93 Georgy Stefula
Deutschland

94 Paps Deutschland

95 Paps Deutschland

96 Karl Kaczmierczak Deutschland

97 Heinrich Schilling Deutschland

98 Miguel G. Vivancos España

99 Rosina Viva Italia

247

100 Orneore Metelli Italia

101 Orneore Metelli Italia

103 Bernardo Pasotti Italia

105 Micheline Boyadjin Belgique

104 Louis Delattre Belgique

106 Léon Greffe Belgique

254

109 Ben Grobben Nederland

110 E. Box Great Britain

111 E. Box Great Britain

112 Scottie Wilson   Great Britain

113 Alfred Wallis Great Britain

116 Niko Pirosmanaschwili UdS

117 Niko Pirosmanaschwili   UdSSR

118 Niko Pirosmanaschwili   UdSSR

119 Niko Pirosmanaschwili   UdSSR

Biographical Notes
and Works Reproduced

ABELARD, Gesnerr
1922   Born in Haiti. Mechanic. Studied painting and sculpture
       at the Industrial School of Port-au-Prince under Humber-
       man Charles, Haitian painter.
1948   Joined Art Center. Began to paint scenes of local Haitian
       life.
       Dining Room. $19^1/_2 \times 15^1/_8''$.
       Stedelijk Museum, Amsterdam. Page 219

ACEVEDO, Felicindo Iglesias y
1898   Born in Orense (Galicia), Spain. Spent eleven years at a
       monastery school in France.
c. 1933   Emigrated to Cuba. Importer of wines and groceries.
1939   Began to paint in spare time. Also active as musician in
       church in Havana, where he lives. Exhibitions in North
       America and Latin America.

ANONYMOUS
       The Pairing Off of the Beasts, 1838. Votive painting,
       Siegertsbrunn, Bavaria. $15^1/_2 \times 14^3/_4''$. Oil on wood.
       Colorplate, page 31
       Votive Painting. Colorplate, page 125
       Betrothal, 1882. Votive painting, Emmersdorf, Lower
       Bavaria. $15 \times 13^5/_8''$. Wood. Bayerisches Landesamt für
       Denkmalpflege, Munich. Page 234

In Gratitude to the Virgin, 1882. Votive painting, Pil-
gramsberg, Lower Bavaria. $12^5/_8 \times 6^3/_4''$. Oil on wood.
Bayerisches Nationalmuseum, Munich. Page 235
Allegory. German folk art, 19th century. Page 237
Prize-winning Dapple-gray Horses, 1907. Painted by
unknown German miner. $18^1/_8 \times 25^1/_4''$.
Private collection, Recklinghausen. Page 238

BAUCHANT, André
1873   Born in Châteaurenault, Indre-et-Loire, France. Market
       gardener. Painted compositions from mythology, land-
       scapes, and flowers.
1914–18   French army, Dardanelles, Greece.
1917   Telemetric draftsman.
1920   Met Ozenfant and Le Corbusier.
1921   First exhibition at the Salon d'Automne; member of the
       Salons.
1927   Commissioned by Diaghilev to design sets for Stra-
       vinsky's *Apollon Musagète*. Exhibition, Galerie Jeanne
       Bucher, Paris.
1937   Included with Rousseau, Bombois, Vivin, and Séraphine
       in the exhibition "Maîtres populaires de la réalité" in
       Paris, Zurich, and (1938) New York.
1958   Died in August.
       Cleopatra's Barge, 1939. $32^1/_8 \times 39^3/_8''$.
       Museum of Modern Art, New York. Colorplate, page 67
       In the Country of Flowers, 1944. $23^5/_8 \times 31^1/_2''$.
       Collection Marcel Mabille, Brussels. Colorplate, page 69
       Adam and Eve. $51^5/_8 \times 35^3/_8''$. Oil on canvas.
       Galerie Charpentier, Paris. Page 169
       Neptune, 1929. $42^1/_8 \times 14^3/_4''$.
       Collection Bignou, Paris. Page 170
       Apotheosis of Homer, 1927. $58^5/_8 \times 85^3/_8''$.
       Collection Bignou, Paris. Page 171

BECKER, Joseph
1841 Born in Sacramento, Calif. Painted landscapes in oil.
1910 Died.
The First Transcontinental Train, 1869. $17^3/_4 \times 24^3/_8''$. Oil on canvas. Thomas Gilcrease Institute of American History and Art, Tulsa, Okla. Page 196

BELIĆ, Cvetan
Painter of peasants, probably in the Voivodina, Yugoslavia. Aside from a few paintings which are signed, nothing is known of this interesting twentieth-century Serbian painter.
Village Wedding, 1937–38. $33^1/_8 \times 45^5/_8''$. Oil on canvas. Collection Siniša Paunovic, Belgrade. Page 232

BENOIT, Rigaud
Born in Haiti. Shoemaker, taxicab driver, and many other occupations. Self-taught. Painted popular scenes, landscapes, and a fresco (Nativity) in the Episcopal Church of Port-au-Prince.
The Spring. Page 216

BIGAUD, Wilson
1931 Born in Port-au-Prince, Haiti. Member of group founded by Hector Hyppolite. Painted mostly regional scenes, often with rich treatment. His *Wedding at Cana* is in the city cathedral, and works of his are in the Museum of Modern Art, New York.
Murder in the Jungle, 1950. $23^7/_8 \times 29^3/_4''$. Museum of Modern Art, New York. Page 217

BLAIR, Streeter
1888 Born in Cadmus, Kans. Lives in Los Angeles, Calif. Worked as waiter during school years, later as drummer in a theater orchestra.
1911 Married. Principal of a school in Junction City. Opened a clothing store but went bankrupt after ten years. Became an antique dealer. When a customer asked to buy a picture he had painted of an old house, he began to paint steadily.
Outing in 1840, 1950. $24 \times 17^7/_8''$. Oil on canvas. Owned by artist. Page 211

BLONDEL, Emile
1893 Born in Le Havre. At sixteen went to sea from Newfoundland. Harbor pilot, bus driver.
1950 Retired. Devoted himself to painting. First exhibition, Galerie Cambacérès, Paris.
Picture of My Life, 1953. Collection I. Moscovitch, Aubervilliers, Seine, France. Page 172

BOËTIUS, Jan Arndt
1809 Born in Wyk, island of Föhr, Germany. Baker. Painted local landscapes, figures in local costumes, and portraits.
1860 Died at Wyk.

BOILAUGES, Fernand
1891 Born in a suburb of Lille, Nord, France.
1949 Discovered by a Paris art dealer, and soon his paintings found an enthusiastic reception.
1955 First exhibition, Kleemann Gallery, New York; in autumn, exhibition in London (Jeffress Gallery). Paintings in many important private collections. However, this success has not changed this simple man. "I can't understand why people admire my paintings," he said in

an interview. "There are so many masterpieces in museums which have never been admired."
Pharmacy at La Pommade, 1956. $14^1/_8 \times 17^3/_4''$. Collection Dr. Martinot, Paris. Page 186

BOMBOIS, Camille
1883 Born in Venarey-les-Laumes, France. His father owned a barge. Spent early years on canals. Worked as a herdsman.
1903 Wrestler in traveling circuses.
1907 Worked on building of Paris subway; night worker in printing plant.
1914 War service.
1922 Article about him by a critic who saw one of his canvases in a Montmartre street exhibit.
1937 First exhibition, "Maîtres populaires de la réalité," Paris. Lives in Paris.
Country Fair Athlete. $51^7/_8 \times 35''$. Musée National d'Art Moderne, Paris. Colorplate, page 167
Nude with Raised Arms. $31^7/_8 \times 23^5/_8''$. Musée National d'Art Moderne, Paris. Page 168

BOUQUET, André
1897 Born in La Varenne-Saint-Hilaire, France. Apprenticed to a mechanic, then to a butcher. Plant superintendent in an airplane factory near Paris.
1914–18 War service in France.
1919 Indochina. After discharge from army, worked for butcher.
1950 Bought first paints. Works at factory and paints in spare time.
1958 First exhibition, Galerie de l'Institut, Paris.
Villeneuve-St.-Georges, 1956. $23^5/_8 \times 28^3/_4''$. Owned by artist. Page 177

BOX, E.
Expulsion from Paradise, 1951. $18^1/_8 \times 16^1/_8''$. Oil on canvas. Collection Dr. Marston Fleming, London. Page 257
Family Group, 1954. $24^3/_8 \times 20^1/_8''$. Oil on canvas. Collection Mrs. John Taylor. Page 257

BOYADJIAN, Micheline
1923 Born in Bruges, Belgium.
1954 Began to paint. First exhibition, Salon de la Jeune Peinture. Married to Russian doctor, lives and works in Brussels.
The Umbrellas, 1957. $21^1/_4 \times 45^1/_4''$. Owned by artist. Page 252

BRAREN, Oluf
1787 Born on island of Föhr, Germany. Teacher at Braderup, Midlum, and Uetersum (Föhr). Nature study led him to painting. Earliest amateur painter in Germany. Family scenes and portraits.
1839 Died of consumption.
Private Wedding, Föhr. $27 \times 19^1/_8''$. Schleswig-Holsteinisches Landesmuseum. Page 236

BRAŠIĆ, Janko
1905 Born in Oparić, Serbia. Lives as a farmer and paints in his native town. While tending sheep and cattle he made drawings, and obtained colors from ripe elderberries.
1933 While helping to build a church, decided to make fresco paintings. Decorated the Orthodox church of his native village with murals.
1936 Siniša Paunović, a writer from Belgrade, visited him at Oparić, encouraged him, and bought some of his paintings.

1937 Exhibited his works at village school.
1945 Resumed painting after war years.
1957 Old and new works in exhibition "Naïve Painters of Yugoslavia," Belgrade.
Battle Between the Serbs and the Turks, 1955–56. 78³/₄×118¹/₈″. Oil on canvas. Owned by artist. Pages 228-229
Dancing the Kolo, 1935. 15³/₈×25⁵/₈″. Oil on canvas. Collection Siniša Paunović, Belgrade. Page 230

BREVEGLIERI, Cesare
1902 Born in Milan, Italy. His parents came from Ferrara. Teacher, clerk.
1928 Devoted himself entirely to painting, as self-taught artist.
1930 Went to Paris on scholarship.
1932 Exhibited at Venice Biennale.
1934 Awarded prize at the Brera Biennale in Milan. Exhibited several works at the 24th Venice Biennale.
1948 Died of cancer.

BUKTENICA, Eugen
1914 Born in Grohota (island of Solta, opposite Split, Croatia). Peasant and fisherman.
1941–44 Prisoner in German concentration camp which he described in epic poem, "The Struggle of the People of Solta."
1946 Began to draw, then to paint.
1950 Met Ante Kastelančić, art teacher at Split, who gave him technical instruction. Since then has painted seascapes and scenes from life of fishermen and coast dwellers.
1957 Represented at exhibition "Naïve Painters of Yugoslavia," Belgrade.

1958 Represented at exhibition "Naïve Painters from Rousseau to the Present," Knokke-le-Zoute, Belgium.
Carnival, 1956. 29¹/₈×19¹/₄″.
Gallery of Primitive Art, Zagreb. Colorplate, page 223
Fishing Boats, 1955. 17³/₄×25⁵/₈″. Oil on canvas.
Gallery of Primitive Art, Zagreb. Page 227

CAILLAUD, Aristide
1902 Born in Moulins, Deux-Sèvres, France. Tended sheep as a boy.
1940–44 Began to paint while prisoner of war.
1949 First exhibition, Galerie Stiebel, Paris.

CERVANTEZ, Pedro
1915 Born in Arizona. Assumed name of Cervantez when he signed his first painting. Discovered and encouraged by R. Vernon Hunter. Employed on WPA Federal Art Project in New Mexico.
1938 Represented at exhibition "Masters of Popular Painting," Museum of Modern Art, New York.

CESETTI, Giuseppe
1902 Born in Tuscany, near Viterbo, Italy. Self-taught. Tendency to romantic-decorative neo-primitive art. Teacher at Accademia, Venice.

CHAMBERS, Thomas
1834 Mentioned as landscapist. Was then living in New York.
1835 Earliest signed painting: *Naval Battle at Puerto Cabello, Venezuela.*
1838–40 Painted seascapes and harbor pictures, called himself marine painter.
1852 Painting: *Agreement between US and the "Macedonian."*
1853 Last painting with his signature. Probable year of death.

CHEVAL, Fernand
1836 Born in Charmes, France. Mail carrier, collected stones during his rounds in the department of Drôme, with which he built his monumental Palais Idéal—the project took 45 years.
1924 Died in Hauterives, Drôme.

COSTA, R.
Active 1840 in the United States. Probably cook aboard whaler. Left behind small signed paintings on wood.

DAVIS, Joseph H.
Began his career at Newfield, Maine.
1832 Earliest of his portraits, of which about 100 watercolors have survived.
1833–34 Views of farms and family portraits at Lebanon, N.H., and North Berwick and Berwick, Maine.
1835 Active at Brookfield, Vt., and in New Hampshire.
1837 Probable year of death.

DECHELETTE, Louis Augustin
1894 Born at Cours, Rhône, France. House painter and plasterer in his youth. Traveled all over France.
1914–18 War service. Worked on inventions.
1940–44 Anti-Fascist paintings.
1942 First exhibition, Galerie Jeanne Bucher, Paris.
1949 Awarded prize.
Outdoor Circus. 15×24″. Owned by artist. Page 176

DELATTRE, Louis
1815 Born at Ghent, Belgium. Mechanic, house painter, banker, photographer.

1865 Flying-machine experiments. Exhibited his paintings in shop windows and cafés. Known locally as "Rubens" and "The Eccentric."
1897 Died at Ghent.
Ascension of Prince Baudouin. 27$^1/_2$×15″.
Collection Franz Hellens, Brussels. Page 252

DEMONCHY, André
1914 Born in Paris. Orphaned by the war, he was raised on a farm in Yonne. Second engineer with railways. Painted trains.
1949 First exhibition, Galerie de Berri, Paris. Catalogue prefaced by André Breton.
Funeral at Semur-en-Auxois, 1957. Owned by artist.
Page 187

DIETRICH, Adolf
1877 Born in Berlingen (Untersee), Switzerland. Son of peasants, as a child he drew pictures in the sand, incised patterns on stones, and molded clay figures, before discovering paint. Laborer, weaver, lumberjack.
1903 Völmy, a painter who lived in Basel, while on a visit to Berlingen encouraged him to paint.
1909 Exhibited in Zurich for first time.
1916 Drawings published in *Buch vom Bodensee.*
1926 Devoted himself almost entirely to painting. Works sold to museums and art dealers. Landscapes, portraits, pictures of animals and flowers.
1957 Died.
Zoo, 1927. 13$^3/_8$×20$^1/_2$″. Oil on canvas.
Galerie Bettie Thommen, Basel. Colorplate, page 133

DUFAUT, Préfète
1923 Born in Jacmel, Haiti. Ship's carpenter. Most of his paintings are views of Jacmel. Mural *(Temptation of the Lord)* in Episcopal Church at Port-au-Prince.

ELMER, Edwin Romanzo
1850 Born in Ashland, Mass. Grew up on a farm, attended village school. Inventor of agricultural machines. For several years supported himself by drawing portraits from photographs.
c. 1895 Went to New York where he studied at National Academy of Design. A year later returned to Ashland, where he painted until his death in 1923.
Memorial Portrait. The Artist, His Wife, and Deceased Daughter, c. 1889. $27^3/_4 \times 33^5/_8$". Oil on canvas.
Smith College Museum of Art, Northampton, Mass. Page 198

EVE, Jean
1909 Born in Somain near Douai, Nord, France. Miner. Apprentice mechanic. Used his first earnings to buy paints. Steelworker, railroad employee, land surveyor, customs agent.
1930 First exhibition, Galerie Alice-Manteau, Paris.
1937 Participated in exhibition "Maîtres populaires de la réalité," Paris. Lives near Giverny, Normandy.

FEJEŠ, Emerik
1904 Born in Osijek, Croatia. Seventh of fourteen children. Grew up in poverty. Button and comb-making apprentice.
1945 Opened secondhand shop at Novi Sad in Voivodina.

1948 Worked as turner and comb maker.
1949 First paintings of city scenes.
1956 Represented in exhibition of primitive artists, Dubrovnik.
1957 In Belgrade.
1958 Represented in exhibition "Naïve Painters from Rousseau to the Present," Knokke-le-Zoute, Belgium. Lives in Novi Sad.
The Garden, 1950. $29^1/_2 \times 32^1/_4$". Gouache.
Commission for Cultural Relations with Foreign Countries, Belgrade. Colorplate, page 121
Subotica, 1950. $22^7/_8 \times 32^1/_4$". Gouache.
Commission for Cultural Relations with Foreign Countries, Belgrade. Page 233

FILIPOVIĆ, Franjo
1930 Born in Hlebine, Croatia. Peasant. Self-taught.
1945 Ivan Generalić saw his drawings and introduced him to painting.
1946 Exhibited with other peasant painters of Hlebine at nearby town of Koprivnica.
1949 Exhibition at Zagreb.
1957 Represented in exhibition "Naïve Artists of Yugoslavia," Belgrade. Lives in his native village, paints in spare time.
In the Reeds, 1957. $12^1/_4 \times 17^3/_4$".
Gallery of Primitive Art, Zagreb. Page 227

FOURÉ, the Abbé
1819 Born at Saint-Thual, France. Worked thirty years on the popular naïve monumental sculptures carved in the cliffs of Rothéneuf near Saint Malo.
1910 Died.

FOUS, Jean

1901 Born in Paris. Has lived a restless life. Sold post cards, trinkets, and self-made picture frames at the Flea Market in Paris.

1944 Began to sell own paintings. First exhibition, Galerie du Dragon, Paris. Now paints landscapes and city views at the Flea Market.
The Flea Market, Vanves, 1945. Collection J. Moscovitch, Aubervilliers, Seine, France. Page 182
The Flea Market, Porte des Lilas, in the Rain, 1945. $20^1/_2 \times 28^3/_4''$. Collection A. Jakovsky, Paris. Page 182

GAŽI, Dragan

1930 Born in Hlebine, Croatia. Began to draw as a child.

1947 Ivan Generalić saw his work, taught him technique of painting on glass.

1952 Exhibited with Hlebine school at Zagreb and Koprivnica.

1957 In Belgrade. Paints only in spare time on farm.

GENERALIĆ, Ivan

1914 Born in Hlebine, Croatia. Began to draw as shepherd.

1930 Met Krsto Hegedušić, who encouraged him to become an artist and instructed him in painting.

1931 Exhibited with Croat group Zemlia.

1936 One-man show in Yugoslavia. Recognized as leader of School of Hlebine.

1953 Exhibited in Paris.

1955 Exhibited in São Paulo, Brazil.

1958 Included in exhibition "Fifty Years of Modern Art," Brussels World's Fair. Lives in his native village, practices art while continuing to be active as farmer.
Burial of Štef Halachek, 1934. $19^5/_8 \times 18^1/_2''$. Oil on canvas. Gallery of Modern Art, Zagreb. Colorplate, page 113
Under the Pear Tree, 1943. $21^5/_8 \times 17^3/_4''$. Oil on glass. Gallery of Modern Art, Zagreb. Page 222
Gypsy Wedding, 1936. $15 \times 20^1/_8''$. Gallery of Modern Art, Zagreb. Page 224

GOURGUE, Jean Enguérrand

1930 Born at Port-au-Prince, Haiti. Began to paint at an early age.

1947 Admitted to Artistic Center, Port-au-Prince. After a primitive period he turned to a realistic style. Possesses a strong feeling for the tragic, and in his work he combines old customs, regional beliefs, and magic rhythms.
Magic Table, 1947. $16^7/_8 \times 20^5/_8''$. Museum of Modern Art, New York. Page 217

GREFFE, Léon

1881 Born in Charleroi, Belgium. Miner, market worker in Paris, janitor.

1945 First exhibition, Galerie du Dragon, Paris. Catalogue prefaced by A. Jakovsky. Obtained contract with art dealer but began to drink.

1949 Died in Paris.
Bastille Day in a Small Town, 1944. $24 \times 19^5/_8''$. Collection A. Jakovsky, Paris. Page 253

GROBBEN, Ben

Fantasy Based on the Tales of Hoffmann, 1959. $9^1/_2 \times 13^3/_4''$. Almelo, Netherlands. Page 256

GUILLÉN, Asilia

1887 Born in Granada, Nicaragua. Embroiderer by profession. Began to paint only a few years ago. Self-taught, but for a time attended art school. Lives in Managua. Exhibits in São Paulo and U.S.

1957   Exhibits at Pan American Union, Washington, D.C.
The Burning of Granada by American Marines.
24⁵/₈ × 28¹/₂″. Owned by artist. Colorplate, page 103

HAMBLETT, Theora
1895   Born in Mississippi. Portraits of children and animals, and a symbolic picture called *Vision*, which attracted attention at exhibition at Knokke-le-Zoute, Belgium, 1958
Vision, 1954. 17⁷/₈ × 48″.
Museum of Modern Art, New York. Page 210

HANSEN, Christian Peter
1803   Born in Keitum, island of Sylt, Germany. Teacher and historian of his native island. Associated with Oluf Braren. Painted watercolors and portraits.
1879   Died in Keitum.

HAYES, George A.
With Bare Fists, c. 1860. 9⁷/₈ × 19⁵/₈″. Oil on cardboard. Collection Edgar William and Bernice Chrysler-Garbisch. Colorplate, page 201

HICKS, Edward
1780   Born in Attleboro, Pa. (now Bensalem). Orphaned at an early age and was raised by a Negro woman.
1793   Apprenticed to a coachmaker.
1800   Opened his own workshop.
1810   Began to travel, preaching at Quaker meetings. Lived puritanically, worked to support his family. Struggled against alcoholism, arousing the hostility of his fellow

Quakers. Because of his preaching activities his business failed, and he took over a farm. This attempt failed, and he returned to his trade. Painted in spare time. His favorite theme was the Peaceable Kingdom, in which the lion lies down with the lamb.
1849   Died.
Cornell Farm, c. 1848. Collection Edgar William and Bernice Chrysler-Garbisch. Colorplate, page 87
Noah's Ark, 1846–48. 26⁵/₈ × 30³/₈″. Oil on canvas. Philadelphia Museum of Art. Page 191

HIRSHFIELD, Morris
1872   Born in a village of Russian Poland. Liked to carve figures out of wood as a boy.
1890   Emigrated to America, got a job in a factory making women's coats. Later manufactured boudoir slippers. After severe illness, retired from business and began to paint.
1936–37   First paintings: *Angora Cat* and *Beach Girl*.
1943   First exhibition, Museum of Modern Art, New York.
1946   Died.
1958   Included in exhibition "Fifty Years of Modern Art," Brussels World's Fair.
Girl Before the Mirror, 1940. 40¹/₈ × 22¹/₄″.
Museum of Modern Art, New York. Colorplate, page 93
Tiger, 1940. 28 × 40″.
Museum of Modern Art, New York. Page 206
Animals in the Forest, 1946. 29⁷/₈ × 39³/₄″.
Sidney Janis Gallery, New York. Page 207
The Artist and His Model, 1945. 48 × 39″. Oil on canvas.
Sidney Janis Gallery, New York. Page 208
Nude with Flowers, 1945. 26 × 20″. Oil on canvas.
Sidney Janis Gallery, New York. Page 209

HOUTMAN, Sipke Cornelis
1871 Born in Dokkum, Netherlands. Worked in bakery. Began to paint at sixty. Self-taught artist. On the back of several paintings, wrote: "The Lord Jesus Christ taught me."
1945 Died in Amsterdam.
Bird Cage, 1936. 13³/₄×15³/₄″. Musée Municipal, Amsterdam. Page 255

HOYER, Thorwald Arenst
1872 Born in Copenhagen, Denmark. Acrobat. Traveled in many countries. Visited museums, busied himself with painting, and has decided to work in the manner of the old masters. His paintings show precision, originality of technique, and a primitive feeling for light effects.
1915 Settled in Chicago.
1936 First one-man show, Findlay Galleries, Chicago.
Inside a Barn, 1937. 30¹/₈×24¹/₄″. Museum of Modern Art, New York. Colorplate, page 99

HYPPOLITE, Hector
1894 Born in St. Marc, Haiti. Voodoo priest. Founded group of naïve painters of Haiti. Encouraged by the Cuban painter Wilfredo Lam and the writer André Breton. Participated in Surrealist exhibitions in Paris. His works are in many collections, including the Museum of Modern Art, New York.
1948 Died in Port-au-Prince.
Composition. Collection Le Centre d'Art, Port-au-Prince, Haiti. Page 219

KANE, John
1860 Born in West Calder, Scotland.

1879 Emigrated to America. Miner, carpenter, steelworker in Pittsburgh, house painter, boxer.
1900 First oils.
1927 Awarded Carnegie prize.
1934 Died in Pittsburgh.
Self-Portrait, 1929. 35×26⁵/₈″. Oil on canvas. Museum of Modern Art, New York (Mrs. John D. Rockefeller, Jr., Fund). Page 204
Touching Up, 1932. 22×28³/₄″. Sidney Janis Gallery, New York. Page 205

KAZMIERCZAK, Karl
1894 Born in Germany. Worker in Thyssen steel mills, Hamborn.
Hard to Resist. 24×26³/₄″. Oil on canvas. Owned by artist. Page 245

KNJAZOVIĆ, Jano
1925 Born in Kovačica, district of Pančevo, Yugoslavia. Peasant.
1944 Self-taught, he began to paint in spare time. Exhibits with group of Kovačica painters in his native village, the towns of the Banat, and the cities of Yugoslavia.
Children Dancing, 1954. 13³/₈×29¹/₂″. Private collection, Belgrade. Page 230

KOCH, Samuel
1887 Born in Warsaw, Poland. Real name: Kochmeister.
1901 Left his family.
1910 Arrived in New York.
1913 Traveled in U.S. Worked at various places, including Ford plant, National Biscuit Company, as stevedore, etc. Back in New York, bought a candy store.

1938 His works shown at the ACA Gallery, Contemporary Art Galleries, and at the exhibition "Unknown American Painters" organized by Sidney Janis. He uses bright, cheerful colors, he says, because the world already has enough troubles.

KOVAČIĆ, Mijo
1935 Born in Gornja Šuma, a village in Croatia. Peasant and cattle breeder.
1953 Began to paint watercolors in spare time. Went to see Generalić, who instructed him in use of oils and the technique of glass painting. His first works in the latter medium acquired by museum in Koprivnica.
1954 First exhibition.
Cow Grazing, 1954. $19^5/_8 \times 27^3/_8$".
Gallery of Primitive Art, Zagreb. Page 225

LAEMMLER, Bartholomäus
1809 Born in Herisau, Switzerland. Most important of Appenzell peasant painters. Painted courtyard scenes with figures and cattle. Works of his, painted in oil on wood, are in the Museum für Völkerkunde, Saint Gallen.
1865 Died.

LAGRU, Dominique
1873 Born in Perrecy-les-Forges, Saône-et-Loire, France. Shepherd, miner.
1949 Began to paint.
1951 First exhibition, Galerie Romi, Paris.
Prehistory: Reptiles, 1956. $25^1/_4 \times 31^1/_2$".
Collection Robert Mock, Basse-Yutz, Moselle. Page 173

LEBDUSKA, Lawrence H.
1894 Born in Baltimore, Md. Grew up in Leipzig, Germany, where he learned to manufacture stained glass.
1912 Went back to the U.S. Worked as decorator. In spare time painted.
1926 Exhibited at Opportunity Gallery of the Art Centre, New York.
1936 One-man show, Contemporary Art Galleries, New York. Lives in New York.
Picking Watermelons, 1940. $44^1/_8 \times 34$".
Collection Harry N. Abrams, New York. Page 215

LEFRANC, Jules
1887 Born in Laval, France (where Henri Rousseau was born). His parents owned a hardware store. Began to paint at an early age, encouraged by Monet. Before Second World War gave up his trade to devote himself solely to painting.
1938 First exhibition, Galerie du Carrefour, Paris.
Railroad Tracks with Eiffel Tower. $51^1/_8 \times 31^7/_8$".
Musée National d'Art Moderne, Paris. Page 174
Detail from *Artist's House*. $39^3/_8 \times 34^1/_4$".
Musée Municipal d'Histoire de l'Art, Saint-Denis, Seine. Page 174
Ship's Propellers. $39^3/_8 \times 34^1/_4$". Musée Municipal d'Histoire de l'Art, Saint-Denis, Seine. Page 175

LITWAK, Israel
1868 Born in Odessa, Russia.
1903 Emigrated to America. Lives in East Flatbush, Brooklyn, N.Y.
c. 1936 Began to paint.

1940   Exhibition, Brooklyn Museum.
Dover, New Jersey, 1947. $22 \times 31^1/_8$". Oil on canvas. Museum of Modern Art, New York (gift of Dr. H. F. Hirschland). Page 215

LOPEZ, José Dolores
c. 1880   Born at Cordova near Santa Cruz, New Mexico. Carved in the traditional manner, holy figures in Spanish colonial style called *santos*. He created his own variations with fantasy. Descended from a family of woodcarvers and worked the soil.
c. 1939   Died.

MARINKOVIĆ, Miroslav
1928   Born in Oparić, Serbia. Peasant. Felt the urge to paint as a boy, but his father discouraged him. His neighbor Brašić, a peasant painter, taught him the technique of oils. Left home so that he could paint in his spare time.

MEHKEK, Martin
1936   Born in Novačka near Gola, Croatia. Peasant.
1957   Participated in exhibition "Naïve Painters of Yugoslavia," Belgrade. Lives in his native village. Paints men at work and scenes from gypsy life.

MEIJER, Salomon, called Sal Meijer
1877   Born in Amsterdam, Netherlands. Diamond cutter by trade.
1914   Began to paint landscapes, still lifes, genre scenes, animals. Lives at Blaricum.
Shelter for Cows. $15^3/_8 \times 23^1/_4$".
Musée Municipal, Amsterdam. Page 254

METELLI, Orneore
1872   Born in Terni, Italy. Shoemaker.
1922   Began to paint in winter evenings as pastimes. Member of Terni town orchestra. Painted mainly his city and its architecture. Many exhibitions and articles by important Italian critics.
1938   Died in Terni.
My Departure for Military Service. $14^5/_8 \times 19^1/_2$". Oil on cardboard. Galerie Wolfsberg, Zurich. Colorplate, page 135
Procession in Front of Terni Cathedral. $25 \times 32^7/_8$". Collection Aurelio de Felice, Acqui Terni. Page 248
The Piazza Victor Emmanuel in Terni. $27^1/_2 \times 39^3/_4$". Collection Aurelio de Felice, Acqui Terni. Page 249
Landscape in Tuscany. $24^3/_8 \times 35^3/_8$". Galerie Wolfsberg, Zurich. Page 250

MILTON, S. F.
Active in United States about 1870.

MIS, Johann
1900   Born in Germany. Employed by Erin Mining Company, Castrop Rauxel. Sunday painter.

MORILL, D.
1860   Active in Connecticut. Genre paintings in oil.
Banjo Player, 1860. $19^1/_8 \times 23^5/_8$". Oil on canvas. Wadsworth Atheneum, Hartford, Conn. Page 197

MOSES, Anna Mary Robertson (known as Grandma Moses)
1860   Born in Eagle Bridge, N. Y., where she lives.
1887   Married Thomas Salmon Moses. The couple rented a farm. Had ten children, of whom five lived.

1930   Began to paint. Louis J. Caldor, a New York collector, bought her first paintings.

1952   Published her memoirs.
Parental House, 1946. 36×48″. Oil on canvas. (Copyright by Grandma Moses Properties, Inc., New York.) Page 212
Christmas at Home, 1946. 18¹/₈×23″. Oil on laminated wood. (Copyright by Grandma Moses Properties, Inc., New York.) Page 213

MRAZ, Franjo

1910   Born at Hlebine, Croatia, into a family of small farmers. At age of thirteen made drawings of people and animals he saw in the fields where he worked.

1930   Met Krsto Hegedušić.

1931   Exhibited with Ivan Generalić, at invitation of Zemlia group.

1935–36   Exhibited at Zagreb Fair and Ulrich Art Galleries, Zagreb. Later studied art, left the Hlebine group. Lives in Belgrade as professional painter.

NAUMOVSKI, Vangel

1924   Born in Ohrid, Macedonia, Yugoslavia. Shepherd, apprentice butcher, gardener, bricklayer, locksmith, coachmaker.

1949   Employed as furniture designer, Ohrid. Self-taught painter. Paints scenes from folk sagas.
Death of Kuzman Ohried, 1956. Oil on lessonite. Page 226

NIKIFOR

c. 1893   Born in the region of Lemkowszeryzna.

1930   Discovered as naïve painter. Works exhibited in Warsaw, Krakow, and other Polish cities.

1955   Fifty works shown in London. Lives in Krynica, Polish resort town, and sells his paintings to visitors there.
Railroad Tunnel, 1955. 8⁷/₈×12³/₈″. Page 260

OBIN, Philomé

1892   Born in Cap Haitien, Haiti. Barber, coffee salesman, interior decorator. Self-taught. Member of Hector Hyppolite's group. Shown in exhibitions in Germany, France, Netherlands, U.S., and Latin America. Lives in Cap Haitien.
Toussaint L'Ouverture Receiving a Message from the First Governor, 1945. 23×16³/₄″.
Collection José Gómez Sicre, Washington. Page 218

O'BRADY (Gertrude MacBrady)

1901   Born in Chicago.

1939   Began to paint in France. In a few years executed fifty works. Interned in concentration camp during Second World War, she could only draw. After 1945 took part in exhibition "American Portraits," Galerie Georges Maratier, Paris.

1948   Jules Supervielle wrote preface to catalogue of her exhibition, Galerie Maeght, Paris.
Washerwomen's Boat in the Seine. Private collection, Paris. Page 179
A la bonne Galette, 1941. 28³/₄×36⁵/₈″.
Collection A. Jakovsky, Paris. Page 180

OCIEPKA, Teofil

1893   Born in Poland. Miner. Paints in his spare time, producing, as does Lagru, mostly fantastic subjects or prehistoric animals. Frequently exhibited in Poland.

1958   Represented in exhibition "Naïve Painters from Rousseau to the Present," Knokke-le-Zoute, Belgium.

PALUŠKA, Martin
1913   Born in Kovačica, district of Pančevo, Yugoslavia. Tractor driver and chief mechanic at local mill. Paints in spare time.
1938   Began to paint in oil. With his friend Sokol, a peasant painter, founded the group of lay painters of Kovačica. Exhibited in the towns of the Banat.
1957   Participated in exhibition "Naïve Painters of Yugoslavia," Belgrade.

PAPS (known as "Maler Paps"—"the Painter Paps")
1882   Born at Naumburg, Hesse, Germany. One of the best-known eye specialists in northern Germany.
1951   Began to paint—recollections of travel, views of ports, flowers, stage scenes.
1958   Represented in exhibition at Knokke-le-Zoute, Belgium. *Ismailia*, 1958. $9^1/_4 \times 7''$. Collection Prof. Kurt Martin, Munich. Colorplate, page 129
        Café Momus, 1958. $13^1/_8 \times 16^1/_4''$.
        Collection Prof. Kurt Martin, Munich. Page 244
        In Flanders I, 1958. $18^3/_4 \times 18^7/_8''$.
        Collection Rudolf Stucken, Port Elizabeth, U. So. Afr. Page 244

PARK, Linton
        Lived in India County, Pa., between 1826 and 1870. Painted genre scenes in oil.
1958   Works exhibited at American Pavilion, Brussels World's Fair.
        Flax Scutching, c. 1860. $31^1/_8 \times 50''$. Oil on linen.
        Collection Edgar William and Bernice Chrysler-Garbisch. Page 192

PARKER, Benjamin
        Portrait of a Little Boy Holding a Watch, 1800–1804. $28 \times 21^1_4.''$ Oil on canvas. Collection Mrs. Charles W. Towbey, Alexandria, Va. Page 189

PASOTTI, Bernardo
1910   Born in Milan, Italy. Worked in father's pharmacy. Painted in spare time. Lives in Milan.
1958   Represented in exhibition at Knokke-le-Zoute, Belgium. *Cathedral of Cremona*. $23^5/_8 \times 29^1/_2''$. Owned by artist. Page 251

PEYRONNET, Dominique-Paul
1872   Born in Talence near Bordeaux, France. Printer.
c. 1920   Began to paint.
1932   Exhibited at the Indépendants and the Salon de L'Ecole Française.
1939   In the catalogue for the exhibition of the Studio Waroline he praised himself.
1943   Died in Paris.
        Reclining Woman. $19^5/_8 \times 24''$.
        Musée National d'Art Moderne, Paris. Colorplate, page 73

PICKETT, Joseph
1848   Born in New Hope, Pa. Traveled with circus, worked as carpenter at country fairs, operated a shooting gallery at New Hope. Later ran grocery store, where he painted. He made his colors out of berries he found in the woods and his brushes from cat hair. He worked for months and years on each work. Only a few of his paintings are known.

1918   Died in New Hope.
        Coryell's Ferry, 1776, and Washington Taking Views,
        1914–18. $37^3/_8 \times 48^7/_8$″. Oil on canvas.
        Whitney Museum of American Art, New York. Color-
        plate, page 194

PIPPIN, Horace
1888   Born in West Chester, Pa. Negro. Began to paint reli-
        gious scenes at ten.
1903   Left school. Had jobs as porter, steelworker, peddler of
        old clothes.
1917   Military service. Went to France with AEF. Influenced
        by Europe.
1930   First oil painting. Until his death painted scenes from
        the life of the American Negro, landscapes, World War
        scenes, religious compositions, and still lifes. Total out-
        put about 100 paintings.
1947   Died in Pennsylvania.
        John Brown on the Way to Execution. Oil on canvas.
        $24 \times 29^7/_8$″. Oil on canvas.
        Pennsylvania Academy of the Fine Arts, Philadelphia.
        Page 202; colorplate, page 203

PIROSMANOSHVILI, Niko (Nikolaus Aslanovich)
1863   Born in Mirzani, Kakhetia, Russia. His father raised
        vegetables. Worked for railroads. Later ran dairy store.
1912   Became known as an artist. Self-taught. Painted the
        life of his people, festivals, still lifes, and folk sagas.
1919   Died in poverty.
        Cow. Page 261
        Wine Tasting. State Museum, Tiflis. Page 262
        Reclining Woman. Page 263
        Banquet. Page 263
        Reclining Woman. Page 263

POSADA, José Guadalupe
1851   Born in Aguascalientes, Mexico.
1873   Principal of school at Léon, Guanajuato.
1878   Moved to Mexico City. Opened engraver's shop and for
        a publisher made illustrations of daily events and draw-
        ings for liturgical publications, advertisements, songs,
        legends, and prayers. He drew critical and progressive
        caricatures for the opposition press.
1913   Died in Mexico City.
1933   Jean Charlot rediscovered the nearly 15,000 prints he
        left and exhibited them.
        Liberal Politician Addressing Crowd, c. 1901. Metal en-
        graving. Page 106

POWELL, H. M. T.
        Self-taught painter active in California c. 1850.

PRIOR, William Matthew
1806   Born in Bath, Maine. As a child drew portrait of neigh-
        bor.
1824   Itinerant portrait painter.
1827   Advertised his services.
1828   Referred to himself as "limner." His portraits fetched
        relatively high prices.
1834   Moved with family to Portland, Maine.
c 1840 Moved to Boston.
1873   Died. Was a follower of William Miller, who in 1843
        preached the Second Coming of Christ.
        Portrait of the Brown Children, c. 1845. $40 \times 35^7/_8$″.
        Collection Mrs. Edith Gregor Halpert, New York. Page 188

RAMHOLZ (Felix Muche)
1868   Born in Querfurt, Germany.
1901   Managed estate.

1916 Began to collect paintings by Picasso, Chagall, Feininger, Marc, Klee, etc.
1928 Began to paint humorous genre scenes.
1947 Died in Ramholz in Bavaria.
Husband. 39×30³/₄″. Oil on canvas. Collection Muche, Krefeld. Page 242

RIMBERT, René
1896 Born in Paris. Post-office clerk. Friend of Max Jacob and Marcel Gromaire.
1918 Began to paint.
1927 First exhibition, Galerie Percier, Paris.
1937 Represented in exhibition "Maîtres populaires de la réalité," Paris and Zurich.
1956 Exhibition Montmorency in Paris, catalogue prefaced by Maximilien Gauthier. Paints street scenes with individual inspiration.
Allegorical Allusion to the Fine Differences between Living Quarters, 1945. Oil on canvas. Collection A. Jakovsky, Paris. Page 178

RINGELNATZ, Joachim (Hans von Bötticher)
1883 Born at Wurzen, Saxony, Germany. Sold newspapers, worked in tobacco shop, decorated display windows, house painter, tourist guide, sailor, naval officer, song writer. Self-taught painter.
1930 Twenty works exhibited at Prussian Academy of Art, Berlin, acquired by the Nationalgalerie and other museums.
1934 Died in Berlin.
1958 Memorial exhibitions in Stuttgart, Berlin, Munich, etc.
Snake Charmer or The Victim, 1926. 18³/₄×15¹/₈″. Oil on linen. Collection Hein Kohn, Hilversum. Page 241

ROSAI, Ottone
1895 Born in Florence, Italy. Contacts with Futurists before First World War.
1915–18 War service.
1919 Painted neo-primitive works. Teaches at the art academy in Florence.

ROUSSEAU, Henri
1844 Born in Laval, France.
1863–64 Army service. Played saxophone in regimental band.
1868 Discharged. Married Clémence Boitard.
1869 Customs clerk.
1870–71 Franco-Prussian war. Rousseau served as noncommissioned officer.
1880 First known paintings.
1884 Death of wife. He applied for pension.
1885 Exhibited for the first time, at Salon des Champs Elysées, Paris.
1886 Exhibited at the Salon des Indépendants. (Except for the years 1899 and 1900, he exhibited there regularly until his death.)
1889 Wrote a vaudeville skit, *A Visit to the Exhibition of 1889.*
1890 Defended by Toulouse-Lautrec. Met Gauguin, Redon, Seurat, Pissarro.
1891 First exotic painting.
1899 Married Joséphine Noury. Wrote play, *A Russian Orphan's Revenge.*
1903 Death of second wife.
1905 Began to exhibit at the Salon d'Automne.
1906 Met Delaunay, Picasso, Apollinaire.
1907 Met Wilhelm Uhde, who published the first monograph on him in 1911.

1908 Famous banquet at the Bateau-Lavoir in Montmartre given by Picasso.
1910 Died in Paris.
Head of Monkey (Zizi). $8^7/_8 \times 6^1/_8''$.
Collection Georges Renand, Paris. Colorplate, page 3
Flowers in Vase, 1909. $18^1/_4 \times 13^1/_4''$.
Albright Art Gallery, Buffalo, N. Y. Colorplate, page 25
Self-Portrait, 1890. $56^1/_4 \times 43^1/_2''$. Oil on canvas.
Narodni Gallery, Prague. Colorplate, page 41
Jadwiga's Dream, 1910. $80^3/_8 \times 118^7/_8''$. Oil on canvas.
Museum of Modern Art, New York (Nelson A. Rockefeller Fund). Colorplate, page 49
Ballplayers, 1908. $45^1/_4 \times 38^1/_4''$. Oil on canvas.
Collection Mrs. Henry D. Sharpe, Providence, R. I. Colorplate, page 53
War, 1894. $44^1/_2 \times 76''$. Oil on canvas.
The Louvre, Paris. Page 158
Country Wedding, 1905. $63^3/_4 \times 44^1/_8''$. Oil on canvas.
Private collection, Paris. Page 159
Sleeping Gypsy, 1897. $50^1/_4 \times 68^7/_8''$. Oil on canvas.
Museum of Modern Art, New York. Page 160
Pierre Loti, 1891. $24 \times 19^5/_8''$. Oil on canvas.
Kunsthaus, Zurich. Page 161
Exotic Landscape, 1905. $78^3/_4 \times 118^1/_8''$. Oil on canvas.
Private collection, Zurich. Page 162
Liberty Inviting the Artists, 1906. $68^7/_8 \times 46^1/_2''$. Oil on canvas. Private collection. Page 163

SAUTER, Aloys
Scarcely anything is known about him. Lived in seclusion in Montreil, near Paris. Left behind only a few paintings. He was a cabinetmaker; his wife composed poems. Died recently.

1958 Represented in exhibition at Knokke-le-Zoute, Belgium.
Hymn to World Peace. $39^3/_8 \times 26^3/_4''$.
Collection Urvater, Brussels. Colorplate, page 79
Cabinetmaker's Workshop, 1931. $27^1/_2 \times 39^3/_8''$.
Collection Félix Labisse, Neuilly-sur-Seine. Page 184

SCHILLING, Heinrich
1898 Born in Germany. Locksmith, Krupp factories, Essen.
Company Docks, 1930. $12^3/_4 \times 16^1/_8''$. Oil on canvas.
Owned by artist. Page 245

SCHUBNEL, Jean
1894 Born in Château-la Vallière, France. Lives in Touraine. Paints pictures of old castles.
1952 First exhibition in Paris, Galerie Palmes.

SERAPHINE (Séraphine Louis, called "Séraphine de Senlis")
1864 Born in Assy, Oise, France. As a child tended sheep. Later moved to Senlis. Worked as cleaning woman. Discovered by Wilhelm Uhde in 1912.
1927 First exhibition, Galerie Quatre Chemins, Paris. Little is known about her life. Her paintings of flowers are to be found in museums and galleries.
1934 Died.
Grapes. $57^1/_2 \times 44^7/_8''$.
Private collection, Paris. Colorplate, page 61
Flowers on Blue Ground. $31^7/_8 \times 23^5/_8''$.
Collection Mme. A. Humbert, Paris. Page 168

SKURJENI, Mato
1898 Born in Veternica, Croatia. Of peasant extraction. House painter. Sent by workingmen's organization to night

school, where he learned the elements of drawing and painting.

1947 Exhibited for the first time with cultural group Vinko Jedjut.

1957 Included in exhibition "Naïve Painters of Yugoslavia," Belgrade.

SMAJIĆ, Petar
1910 Born in Donji Dolac near Split, Croatia. Lives in Ernestinovo near Osijek. Worked as coachmaker. Carved ornamental heads for guslas. Encouraged by art lovers.
1935 Devoted himself more fully to wood carving. His works were shown at exhibitions of naïve artists in Yugoslavia.
1958 Works shown at Yugoslav Pavilion, Brussels World's Fair.

SNOW, Jenny Emily
1845 Born in Hinsdale, Mass. Further data are lacking. She worked in oils, painting landscapes and Biblical subjects.

SOKOL, Jano
1909 Born in Kovačica, district of Pančevo, Yugoslavia.
1938 Met the peasant painter Martin Paluška in the library of Kovačica.
1952 Group of Kovačica painters founded.
1953 Advised by painter Trumič of Pančevo to stop copying and to paint his own scenes of peasant life.
Wedding Procession, 1956. 22$^7/_8 \times$ 38$^5/_8''$.
Commission for Cultural Relations with Foreign Countries, Belgrade. Page 231

SPIELBICHLER, Franz A.
1899 Born in Trübenbach, Lower Austria.

1917 Military service.
1919 Miner.
1939 Soldier and later prisoner of war in Russia.
1945 Employed as file cutter by Furtholf plant in Lower Austria. In his spare time paints, mostly local landscapes.

STEFULA, Georgy
1913 Born in Hamburg, Germany. Father was Hungarian and mother was French.
1949 Works shown for the first time at Great Exhibition, Munich.
1952 Included in exhibition "Peintres naïfs," Galerie Wolfsberg, Zurich, and in Museum am Ostwall, Dortmund.
1954, 1956, 1958 Works shown in Zurich and other cities.
The Bird Peddler, 1956. 21$^1/_4 \times$ 28$^3/_4''$. Oil on canvas.
Galerie Wolfsberg, Zurich (exhibition 1958). Page 243

STOCK, Joseph Whiting
1815 Born in Springfield, Mass.
1826 Badly injured in accident, crippled for life. Eventually able to sit up in wheel chair.
1832 Began to study art and to paint.
1842 Began diary.
1855 Died at Springfield, Mass.

STOLNIK, Slavko
1929 Born in Voća Donja near Varaždin, Croatia. As a schoolboy made little figures from clay, wood, etc.
1948 As a member of a youth group helped to build highway from Belgrade to Zagreb. Painted watercolor illustrations for group's news posters.
1949 Army service. Made drawings of fellow soldiers.

1952   Joined the People's Militia, where his artistic pursuits were encouraged.
1954   Met the painter Krsto Hegedušić, who gave him instruction.
1955   First of a series of exhibitions.

STRAKUŠEK, Jano
1926   Born in Kovačica, district of Pančevo, Yugoslavia. Farm hand. Fought in Serbian resistance movement during Second World War, when he began to paint.
1946   Bricklayer.
1952   Contractor in his village. Exhibits with the Kovačica group.

STRYGEL, Hans
1916   Born in Vienna, Austria. Apprenticed to a carpenter. During periods of unemployment painted and made silhouettes which he sold in the streets.
1939   War service. Poland, France, Bay of Biscay, Russia (Voronezh front).
1943   War prisoner.
1947   Repatriated. Now carpenter in Baden, near Vienna.
1958   Awarded prize for self-portrait at the exhibition of Austrian Federation of Labor, "Talente erweckt—entdeckt."

SULLIVAN, Patrick J.
1894   Born in Braddock, Pa.
1916   Enlisted in army. Commissioned officer.
1919   Discharged. Married. Ethiopian war inspired his first pictures.
1937   Became known.

1938   Works exhibited in Museum of Modern Art, New York. Lives in Wheeling, W. Va.
The Fourth Dimension, 1938. 27$^1/_2$×30$^3/_8$".
Collection Sidney Janis Gallery, New York. Page 210

THEGEN, Carl Christian
1883   Born in Oldesloe near Lübeck, Germany. Worked for butcher.
1902   Clown in "Old Belli's" circus, cared for animals in the Hagenbeck circus, and later operated his own merry-go-round.
1914–18   With army, services of supply, in Russia and France.
1918–39   Tramp, part-time worker, butcher, gardener, farm hand, etc.
c. 1933   Began to paint.
1939   Sent to nursing home.
1947   Discharged, part-time worker. Painted in his spare time.
1955   Died in poverty near Oldesloe.
Interior of a Farmhouse. 29$^1/_2$×42$^1/_8$".
Collection Hans-Friedrich Geist, Lübeck. Page 239

TRILLHAASE, Adalbert
1859   Born at Erfurt, Germany. Apprenticed to businessman. Failed in several business ventures. Read a great deal, particularly history books and Bible.
1918   Began to paint. Mother Ey, owner of a café near the Düsseldorf Academy, who later ran a small gallery, gave him his first exhibitions.
1924   A number of works included in Gesolei exhibition, Düsseldorf.
1933   Forbidden to paint as a "degenerate" artist.
1936   Died at Königswinter.

1939   First large exhibition, Maratier, Paris.
        Casting Out the Devils near Gerasa. 19⁵/₈×43¹/₄″. Oil on canvas. Galerie Chichio-Haller, Zurich. Page 240

TYTGAT, Edgar
1879   Born in Brussels. Spent early years in Bruges. His father was a lithographer, and he learned to draw in his workshop. Studied at Academy of Fine Arts, Brussels.
1907   Settled at Watermael near Brussels. Many paintings rejected from exhibitions.
1913–14 First exhibitions, Ghent and Brussels. Fled to London during First World War, stayed there till armistice, then lived at Woluwe-Saint-Lambert near Brussels.
1957   Died in Brussels.
        He began as an Impressionist, then shifted to a personal naïve style, characterized by pure and delicate use of color.

URTEAGA, Mario
1875   Born in Cajamarca, Peru.
1934   First exhibition.
1937   First prize, International Competition, Viño del Mar, Chile.
1955   Honored by Institute for Contemporary Art, Lima. Museum of Modern Art, New York, acquired one of his paintings.
1957   Died.
        Burial of an Illustrious Man, 1936. 23×32¹/₂″. Museum of Modern Art, New York. Colorplate, page 105

UTRILLO, Maurice
1883   Born in Paris, son of Susanne Valadon.
1899   Apprenticed to a banker. Treated for alcoholism in nursing home.

1902   Began to paint.
1908–10 "White period," mixture of naïve and Post-Impressionist elements.
1912   In nursing home at Saunois.
1923   Exhibition Bernheim-Jeune, which made him world famous.
1927   "Picture post-card" period.
1955   Died.

VAN HYFTE, Camille
1886   Born in Ertvelde, Belgium. Farmer, horse butcher, took part in bicycle races.
1951   Began to paint. Decorated walls of his house, carved, etc.
1955   Exhibition, Galerie de l'Institut, Paris. Preface to catalogue by A. Jakovsky. Lives in Paris suburb.
        Interior with Flowers. Collection Mlle Edmonde Charles-Roux, Paris. Colorplate, page 141

VAN WEERT, Jan
1871   Born in Hertogenbosch, Netherlands. Horse trainer, travel agent, hotel owner, rider at horse shows in Paris, London, etc. Began to paint in his seventies, after the Second World War. Lives in Düsseldorf.

VEČENAJ, Ivan
1920   Born in Gola, Croatia. Son of poor parents. After farm work he drew and painted pastels.
1954   Began to paint in oil. On winter nights also tried his hand at sculpture. Works shown at exhibition of peasant painters at Koprivnica and, in 1957, at exhibition "Naïve Painters of Yugoslavia," Belgrade.
        Rest, 1954. 18¹/₈×20¹/₂″. Gallery of Primitive Art, Zagreb. Page 229

VELASQUEZ, Antonio J.
1906　Born in Caridad, Honduras. Telegraph worker, barber, mayor of San Antonio de Oriente, a village in the hills of Honduras which he often used as a motif.
1933　Began to paint oils—altar decorations, flags for processions, landscapes, compositions.
1951　Works exhibited at the Hispano-American Biennale, Madrid.
1954　First one-man show, Pan American Union, Washington. Awarded prize for Christmas cards.
San Antonio de Oriente, 1957. $27^1/_2 \times 36^3/_8$".
Owned by artist. Page 221

VIRIUS, Mirko
1889　Born in Djelekovac, Croatia. Prisoner of war in Russia during First World War.
1936　Established contact with Generalić and Mraz of Hlebine group. Exhibited with this group. Painted scenes of peasant life.
1943　Died in concentration camp of Zemun.
Included in exhibitions, São Paulo, 1955, and Knokke-le-Zoute, 1958. Most of his works are in the Gallery of Primitive Art, Zagreb.
Wedding, 1938. $25^5/_8 \times 18^1/_2$". Oil on canvas.
Gallery for Contemporary Art, Rijeka. Page 231

VIVA, Rosina
1900　Born on the island of Capri, Italy.
1943–45　Refugee in Switzerland. Began to paint Italian landscapes out of homesickness.
1946　Went back to Naples.
Wedding at the Foot of Vesuvius, 1953. $29^1/_8 \times 22^7/_8$".
Collection R. Vautier-Viva, Naples. Page 247

VIVANCOS, Miguel G.
1897　Born in Mazarrón, Murcia, Spain. Chauffeur, dock worker, house painter, glazier, miner.
1936　Commandant of Puigcerda during Spanish Civil War. After the end of the war fled to France, and spent five years in concentration camp.
1944　Went to Paris after Liberation. Painted on silk. Began to paint naïve works. Picasso acquired one of these.
1950　Exhibition, Galerie Mirador, Paris. Preface to catalogue by André Breton.
Still Life with Pheasant. $21^1/_4 \times 28^3/_4$". Oil on canvas.
Owned by artist. Page 246

VIVIN, Louis
1861　Born in Hadol in the Vosges, France. Son of a schoolteacher.
1879–1922　Post-office clerk.
1889　Showed *The Pink Flamingo* at an exhibition of post-office clerks. Moved to Paris.
1922　Retired on pension. Devoted himself entirely to painting.
1925　Met Wilhelm Uhde, who encouraged and supported him. In the last years of his life, had paralysis of right arm and tongue.
1936　Died in Paris.
Versailles. $17^3/_4 \times 23^5/_8$".
Collection Möring, Paris. Colorplate, page 63
Port. $15 \times 21^5/_8$". Private collection, Paris. Page 164
Wild Boar Hunt. $21^1/_4 \times 28^3/_4$".
Private collection, Paris. Page 165

WALLACE, John
c. 1860　Born in Canada. Tribal artist of the Haida Indians (northwestern coast of Canada). Carved totem poles containing certain elements of portraiture.

WALLIS, Alfred
1855   Born in Devonport, England. Later went to sea.
1892   Fisherman at St. Ives, Cornwall.
1928   Began to paint in his seventies. Discovered and encouraged by Ben Nicolson and Christopher Wood. In the 1930s his paintings on cardboard and wood were shown in London galleries.
1942   Died in very modest circumstances in St. Ives.
        The Bridge. Collection Peter Runyon, St. Ives, Cornwall. Page 259

WHITE, Emil
        Strangers of the World, Unite. $11 \times 15^3/_8''$. Watercolor. Private collection. Page 214
        Stranger Here Myself. $9 \times 11^3/_8''$. Watercolor. Owned by artist. Page 214

WILLIAMSON, Clara McDonald
1875   Born in Iredell, Tex. Grew up among settlers and cowboys and herded longhorn cattle and wild horses.
1943   Began to paint.
1946   Exhibition in Dallas Museum of Fine Arts.

WILSON, Scottie
1890   Born in Glasgow, Scotland, into a working-class family. His drawings have calligraphic and visionary qualities. His work suggests the totemistic influence of American Indians. He participated in the exhibition of fantastic art in Basel.
        Quiet Village in the Mountains. $21^5/_8 \times 20^1/_2''$. Gouache. Collection Urvater, Brussels. Page 258

Index of Names

DATE DUE			
JAN 6 '64			
APR 15 '65			
MR 6 '67			
MY 12 '67			
MY 16 '69			
MY 24 '69			
MY 8 '72			
OC 6 '87			